D1557774

A PRIMER FOR TEACHING WOMEN, GENDER, AND SEXUALITY IN WORLD HISTORY

—— Ten Design Principles ——

Merry E. Wiesner-Hanks and
Urmi Engineer Willoughby

DUKE UNIVERSITY PRESS
Durham and London
2018

© 2018 Duke University Press
All rights reserved
Printed in the United States of America
on acid-free paper ∞
Text designed by Jennifer Hill
Typeset in Garamond Premier Pro
by Copperline Books

Library of Congress Cataloging-in-Publication Data
Names: Wiesner, Merry E., [date] author. |
Willoughby, Urmi Engineer, [date] author.
Title: A primer for teaching women, gender, and
sexuality in world history / Merry E. Wiesner-Hanks
and Urmi Engineer Willoughby.
Description: Durham : Duke University Press, 2018. |
Series: Design principles for teaching history | Includes
bibliographical references and index.
Identifiers: LCCN 2018008255 (print)
LCCN 2018009567 (ebook)
ISBN 9781478002475 (ebook)
ISBN 9781478000785 (hardcover : alk. paper)
ISBN 9781478000969 (pbk. : alk. paper)
Subjects: LCSH: Women's studies. | Sex—History—
Study and teaching (Secondary) | Sex—History—Study
and teaching (Higher) | History—Study and teaching
(Secondary) | History—Study and teaching (Higher)
Classification: LCC HQ1180 (ebook) |
LCC HQ1180 .W54 2018 (print) | DDC 305.4—dc23
LC record available at https://lccn.loc.gov/2018008255

Cover art: Silvia Heyden, *Hurricane*, twentieth
century (detail). Silk and linen, 80.75 × 94.25 inches.
Collection of the Nasher Museum of Art at Duke University,
Durham, North Carolina. Gift of Mary D. B. T. Semans and
James H. Semans, M.D.; 1976.101.1. © Silvia Heyden
Estate. Photo by Peter Paul Geoffrion.

Contents

A Primer for Teaching Women, Gender, and Sexuality in World History

DESIGN PRINCIPLES
FOR TEACHING HISTORY
A series edited by Antoinette Burton

THIS BOOK AND HOW TO USE IT

Courses in women's history began to be offered in the 1960s in response to the women's liberation movement, and courses on the history of sexuality in the 1970s in response to the gay and lesbian rights movement. They have changed shape since then as new perspectives developed—gender, cultural studies, queer theory, intersectionality, transfeminism—but remain a common part of the array offered by history departments, women's and gender studies programs, and sometimes by LGBTQ programs. Departments reorganizing their undergraduate program to move away from a nation-based curriculum to one that is more thematic often include gender and sexuality as one of their themes. Thus historians hired in positions defined geographically and chronologically may be asked to teach a general course in gender or sexuality, or one about women or gender in "their" area or time period, whether or not they have training or background in gender studies. Women's and gender studies faculty may be expected to teach a course in history, even though their women's studies graduate training featured little or no history, or their graduate training was actually in literature, philosophy, sociology, or some other field. Faculty hired as lecturers, visiting professors, ad hoc instructors, or in the other types of contingent positions that now make up more than half the teaching staff at many colleges and universities may be asked or required to teach anything the department needs.

This primer is designed to assist new and veteran instructors in all these situations to develop more coherent and thoughtful courses in the history of women, gender, and/or sexuality from a global perspective, in today's teaching environment for today's students. It is also designed for those who want to integrate gender and sexuality more fully into general world history courses. In teaching these topics there is no canon of what absolutely must be taught, leaving much up to the instructor, which is both liberating and terrifying. At the same time, instructors are often restricted by various institutional requirements about "shared learning goals," "course objectives," "learning outcomes," or similar schema that impose a set template, often with little regard for history as a discipline. This primer provides guidance for navigating within these two extremes to create meaningful courses. It aims to present ten general design principles, incorporated into the chapter titles, beginning with setting goals in chapter 1 and ending with connecting with the community in chapter 10. Each chapter includes a few detailed examples of best practices and practical strategies. These examples range widely in time and space, as appropriate for designing courses with a global perspective, but the issues and examples are also pertinent to courses that focus on a single region or even a single country. The ten chapters of the primer are organized into three sections. The first section discusses designing a course from the ground up, the second is about modifying existing courses because of changes in the field or in modes of instruction, and the third reviews common challenges and opportunities. Whatever your specific aims, however, we urge you to read the whole book, as suggestions about materials and assignments are threaded throughout. Each chapter can help you choose from the richness of available published and online materials, and most present ideas about possible course activities based on these.

We represent two different generations of historians, with very different training and experiences in the field, which have shaped our perspectives.

Merry: I have never actually taken a course in women's, gender, or sexuality history, or in world/global history. My first experience with women's history courses was as a graduate teaching assistant in the late 1970s, for a course in medieval women's history taught by an ad hoc instructor at the University of Wisconsin–Madison. I was writing a dissertation on working women in sixteenth-century Nuremberg, and a few other graduate students were also writing dissertations about women, but none of the sixty-plus tenured or tenure-track members of the history department (two of them women) were interested in teaching women's history, nor did they know much about it. In my first teaching position, for which I was hired to teach all of European history, I occasionally taught a European women's history course, but more often a course in U.S. women's history, although I had taken no U.S. history at all in graduate school. I got ideas from asking people who did know what they were doing, many of whom I had met at the Berkshire Conference on the History of Women, for their suggestions, materials, and syllabi, which they sent me as mimeographed or dittoed sheets of paper, now quaint artifacts from olden times. When I moved to a larger department my colleagues who were U.S. historians handled that course (thankfully), but my European women's history course evolved into a course on women and gender as I tried to keep up with an exploding field. In the 1990s I became the director of the Center for Women's Studies and developed a course in interdisciplinary feminist theory, though I had never taken a course with any of those three words in its title. Again help from my friends and colleagues, now in many departments, was essential. Somewhat later different friends and colleagues taught me—and other doubters in women's studies—how to combine feminist pedagogy and online teaching.

I moved into world/global history in much the same way. About 2000, a colleague who specialized in modern Chinese history and I decided that our separate survey courses in Eastern civilization and Western civilization did not reflect the world that we or our students lived in. We designed an introductory world history sequence, for which there were splendid models elsewhere, now available on screens as well as on pieces of paper. We brought in several experienced instructors and world/global scholars as consultants, as the department was "going global" in other undergraduate and graduate courses as well. My very first world history survey class was on September 4, 2001, and included an explanation of why the University of Wisconsin–Milwaukee was now teaching world history. Exactly one week later my explanation no longer seemed quite so necessary. I have been teaching the first semester of this ever since, along with upper-level thematic and graduate courses with a global perspective. My European women's and gender history course still has Europe in the title, but as a result of moving into global history in other courses and in my own research, this is a Europe that is bigger and more connected to the rest of the world than it was when I started teaching the course. Materials available in published form or online for teaching this course or my other courses are now so plentiful that it is hard even to get an overview, so my requests for help are generally for guidance through the riches rather than for sharing a rare treasure, though sometimes I still get the latter.

Urmi: Unlike Merry, I started college and graduate school when studies of world/global history and women, gender, and sexuality were fairly common in many programs. As an undergraduate in the late 1990s, I took courses in women's history, feminist studies, and human sexuality. I completed my graduate coursework in the early 2000s at the University of California, Santa Cruz. The university had been a pioneer in women's, gender, and LGBT studies since the 1970s, and I was fortunate to work alongside numerous scholars in the field. My primary training in graduate school was in world history, and I worked closely with Edmund Burke III at the Centre for World History. I continued my training as a postdoctoral fellow at the University of Pittsburgh's World History Center. When I narrowed my interests to write a dissertation, I grew increasingly interested in environmental history as a broad way to frame my research on health and disease in the nineteenth-century Atlantic world.

My broad and somewhat random interests in seemingly unconnected histories led me to pursue world history. I have had experience teaching world history at several institutions, ranging from a small liberal arts college to large state universities. I have enjoyed the opportunity to design various versions of world history surveys at different scales. Along with conventional periodizations, I designed courses that focused on the long nineteenth century and courses that approached human history as a whole.

At the University of Pittsburgh, I became interested in exploring thematic world history courses, such as courses on the environment, food, slavery, and women, gender, and sexuality.

My interest in women, gender, and sexuality has always been present, but not always at the forefront of my research and teaching interests. I became concerned with the separation of women's studies and feminist studies from world history, especially in the classroom. Because issues of women, gender, and sexuality form an essential part of any history, I found ways to incorporate them into my world history and other thematic courses. I have found that virtually any course could be transformed to focus on issues of women, gender, and sexuality. A thematic course on food, or a regionally focused course, can be turned to focus on the experiences of women, or to use gender as an analytical frame in understanding dynamics of power and culture in shaping history.

I taught my first course on women and gender, titled "Gender in World History," at the University of Pittsburgh in the spring of 2015, and I found it to be one of the most intellectually challenging and stimulating experiences of my career. When I began designing the course, I started by looking through my syllabi and pulling out lessons and readings on relevant topics. It was instructive to see the ways that I had been incorporating women, gender, and sexuality into my courses, and what themes dominated. I found it difficult to avoid essentializing the experiences of women, or framing courses as narratives of progress. I became very aware of the challenges of balancing narratives of women's agency and oppression. Like Merry, I turned to my colleagues for assistance in areas outside of my fields of specialization. I became interested in including as many perspectives as possible into my approach. I grew especially interested in learning how scholars of China, South Asia, and the Islamic world approached issues of women and gender compared with historians of Europe and North America. Conversations with my colleagues were integral to finding ways to structure a course that considered women, gender, and sexuality studies from a global historical perspective. I have continued to develop this course at Murray State University, and I look forward to improving it by working with colleagues with different research specialties than mine. Next on my agenda is to collaborate with colleagues to team-teach the course. This would serve as a practical way for educators to integrate wider perspectives into their own syllabi.

Returning to our joint voice: Despite the growth of both world/global history and women, gender, and sexuality history over the last several decades, challenges in teaching these remain, and the advice in this primer grows out of our own experiences facing them. Voice is a key issue in both these fields, as both have sought to give voice to individuals and groups that have been silenced, ignored, or muted, so we thought it important to explain how voice works in this book. We have pooled our experiences within this joint writing project, so most of the time "we" means the two of us, though occasionally "we" is the larger group of "we historians of women, gender, and sexuality" or the even larger group "we teachers of history." Where we write about the premodern, Merry's expertise is the most evident, and where we write about the modern, Urmi's, though both of us teach across a long span of time so our knowledge is interwoven. Occasionally we speak in a singular voice to describe specific examples and classroom strategies, signaling this with "I (Merry)" or "I (Urmi)." "You" is always our envisioned reader.

We have conceived this primer in the spirit of all those who have helped us conceptualize, structure, and improve our courses, as a first hand of assistance, though certainly not a substitute for developing your own network for advice and support. Designing a new course or revising an existing one to keep up with developments in research and theory, or with changes in our students or the world, is challenging, but it is also fun.

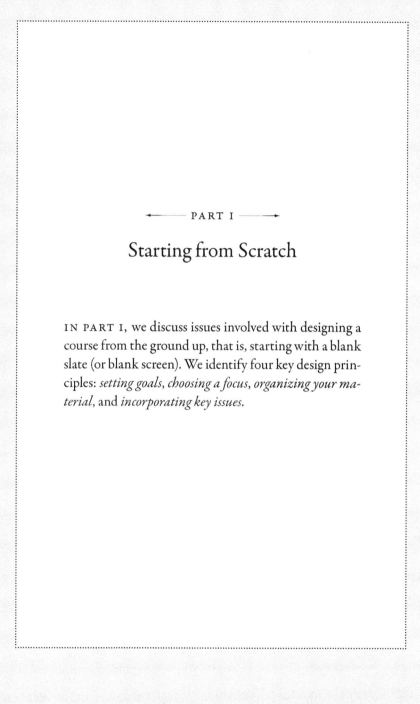

—— PART I ——

Starting from Scratch

IN PART I, we discuss issues involved with designing a course from the ground up, that is, starting with a blank slate (or blank screen). We identify four key design principles: *setting goals, choosing a focus, organizing your material*, and *incorporating key issues*.

Setting Goals

WHY TEACH WOMEN'S, GENDER, OR SEXUALITY HISTORY?

WE SEE *SETTING GOALS* as the first design principle for both philosophical and practical reasons. Before teaching any course, think about why you are doing this. What's the point? Why spend your time and energy on this as opposed to something else? Having a clear answer will allow you to weather the inevitable moment in any semester when "why am I doing this?" will pop into your head. (This often happens after students turn in their first assignment.) Along with lifting you out of existential despair, a well-thought-out answer has practical benefits. Most departments or programs today require syllabi to contain a statement about course goals and learning outcomes. These should come from your underlying philosophy about what you hope to accomplish in the course, that is, what you want students to know, understand, and be able to do when they have finished.

Just as your course is embedded in a larger array of courses offered in a history department, women's and gender studies program, humanities department, LGBTQ program, or some other unit, the question that is the subtitle to this chapter is part of a larger question: Why teach history? Thus before you zero in on this course, you may want to craft an answer to this more general question, which every one of us who teaches history would answer slightly differently. We want students to learn about, gain familiarity with, discover, acquire knowledge of, come to understand (or some other phrase describing this process) an era of the past, generally for some reason, though often the latter is fairly vague. For example, a general world history survey might note that students will "gain familiarity with world history over a broad sweep of time, including issues of periodization, key themes, world regions, and processes of continuity and change in order to understand the varieties and complexities of the human experience throughout time and around the world." Short statements like this are then augmented by lists of more specific goals and learning objectives related to the material covered in the course.

Along with learning historical content, we generally also want students to develop historical thinking skills. Again each of us would lay these out slightly differently, based on our sense of what historical thinking involves. Here is one description:

> Historical thinking requires understanding and evaluating change and continuity over time and making appropriate use of relevant historical evidence to answer questions and develop arguments about the past. It involves going beyond simply asking "what happened when" to evaluating why and how events occurred and processes unfolded. It involves finding and assessing historical sources of many different types to understand the contexts of given historical eras and the perspectives of different individuals and groups within geographic units that range from the local to the global. Historical thinking is a process of chronological reasoning, which means wrestling with issues of causality, connections, significance, and context with the goal of developing credible explanations of historical events and processes based on reasoned interpretation of evidence.[1]

The American Historical Association (AHA) has developed a list, called the "History Discipline Core," with many of the same skills, along with those involved in communicating historical knowledge, such as being able to "craft well-supported historical narratives, arguments, and reports of re-search findings in a variety of media for a variety of audiences" and "revise analyses and narratives when new evidence requires it."[2]

There are many other lists and descriptions around as well, and embed-ded in most of these is the idea that such skills are not simply useful for one history class, but things we hope will become habits of mind to be applied to the world at large. Habits of mind in the descriptions above include "understanding the varieties and complexities of the human experience . . . and the perspectives of different individuals and groups," and knowing that explanations should be "based on reasoned interpretation of evi-dence." The AHA History Discipline Core opens with the statement that "history is a public pursuit . . . essential to active citizenship" and includes such habits of mind as developing "positions that reflect deliberation, co-operation, and diverse perspectives" and applying "historical knowledge and historical thinking to contemporary issues."

If you have not developed your own general statement about your goals in teaching history, we recommend that you do that first, as you can use it on all your syllabi. Then you can turn to the only-slightly-narrower ques-tion about why you are teaching women's, gender, and/or sexuality history, either as an aspect of your world history course or as a stand-alone course. What is it that you want students to come to understand, and are there specific skills or habits of mind you hope they will develop? In thinking about this, it might be useful to review how and why the history of women, gender, and sexuality developed as scholarly fields, because this shapes what most of us hope to accomplish by teaching these today.

Fifty years ago the question would have been shorter and simpler. Q: Why teach women's history? A: Because women are almost never included in history courses, other than the very few, such as Indira Gandhi, who cannot be avoided and because focusing on women in every field of knowl-edge is an important feminist enterprise that will lead to social transfor-mation. Teaching women's history was a political act, undertaken initially through student-led teach-ins and workshops or by faculty who were also activists in the women's movement. Women are part of history, they asserted, and history that does not include women is incomplete. There are debates about what was the first actual course, but Gerda Lerner's 1963 course in U.S. women's history at the New School for Social Research is a prime contender for this honor. By the late 1960s there were informal and formal courses at a number of colleges and universities, and by the late 1970s, hundreds of colleges and universities in various parts of the world offered courses in women's history, and many had separate programs in women's studies. At this time most college history courses were nationally or regionally specific, so women's history courses were as well. The people who taught women's history—most, but not all, of them women— gathered and shared materials, and once the market was large enough publishers began issuing collections of articles, source readers, surveys, and other materials designed for the classroom.

Forty years ago the gay liberation movement provided a similar answer to a similar question. Q: Why teach the history of sexuality? A: Because sexuality, especially homosexuality, is almost never mentioned in history courses, and because studying same-sex relations in the past can provide insights for those seeking to bring about change today. The first course on the history of sexuality appears to have been taught in 1970 (several different universities claim theirs was the first), and the number expanded steadily after this, though not as explosively as in women's history. A few programs in gay and lesbian studies were founded, and more were established in the 1990s and early 2000s (by which time the standard title was LGBT) when worries that such programs would be controversial with alumni donors or government officials abated a bit. Most early courses on the history of sexuality focused exclusively on the West (sometimes noting this, though often not), starting with classical Athens and ending with the Stonewall riots, although a few included some discussion of other cultures, especially East and South Asia. The people who taught these courses—most, but not all of them, gay and lesbian themselves—also gathered and shared materials, though mainstream publishers were not as eager to produce materials for the classroom as they were in women's history, and works issued by small independent publishers remained crucial as teaching materials.

Many of the courses that were created in the 1960s and 1970s are still on the books. The University of Wisconsin–Milwaukee, for example, regularly offers a one-semester, very broad overview titled "Family and Sex Roles in the Past"; a one-semester undergraduate course in U.S. women's history; a two-semester course in European women's history; and a one-semester course on the history of homosexuality. Similar patterns can be found in many places, although the courses themselves are often quite different from what they were originally. Challenged by women of color about an overemphasis on the experiences of white women, scholars and teachers of women's history have increasingly emphasized differences among women along many lines—race, class, ethnicity, economic status, nationality, religion, ability, sexual orientation, age, location, and so on—and structured their courses accordingly. Many picked up on an idea that originated with the activist Combahee River Collective in 1977 that "the major systems of oppression are interlocking" to examine what in 1989 the legal scholar and critical race theorist Kimberlé Crenshaw termed "intersectionality": the concept that the nature of oppression is multiplicative rather than additive.[3] They also incorporated ideas that originated in the history of colonialism and its theoretical branch, postcolonial theory, in which questions of identity and the cultural construction of difference have also been central areas of inquiry. Postcolonial scholars such as Chandra Mohanty and Gayatri Spivak were particularly influential in calling for a focus on relationships of hierarchy and oppression, and for placing these within the global context of colonization and imperialism rather than viewing them as regionally specific.[4] Scholars and teachers in women's history responded to critical race theory and postcolonialism by threading concepts of difference, otherness, hierarchy, and hegemony throughout their courses in an attempt to be attentive to the varied ways that power operates rather than simply adding units on various subordinate groups.

The originators of these courses might view the fact that they are still being taught at all decades later as a mark of their failure, however. Almost as soon as women's history courses were created, faculty and students debated their future. Should women's history be taught separately, or did doing so reinforce the idea that women's history is not "real" history? Was this freedom or a ghetto? Should those interested in the field instead work on ensuring that material on women was in every course, what was then termed "mainstreaming"? Was mainstreaming likely to be transformative, or would it be a watering down of feminist principles? To many, both strategies seemed valuable, and women's history was mainstreamed to some degree. Some faculty who did not generally teach women's history began adding a lecture or two to their courses, and those who *did* teach women's history began to get full-time positions, so women were included in all their courses from the beginning. Information on women began to show up in textbooks for general history courses, first often in sidebars and boxes and then inserted into the actual narrative. This was generally a matter of fitting women into familiar historical categories, such as nations, historical periods, and intellectual movements—an approach women's historians sarcastically labeled "add women and stir"—but occasionally it led to a slight rethinking of the way courses and textbooks were organized and structured. Sexuality was more controversial to mainstream, although some courses and textbooks began to cover certain topics, such as prostitution, sexually transmitted diseases, and even same-sex relations. But to most people committed to the history of sexuality, such mainstreaming efforts were pretty paltry, and the need for separate courses remained.

A different type of mainstreaming also began in the 1980s, when scholars familiar with studying women increasingly began to discuss the ways in which systems of sexual differentiation affected both women and men, using the word "gender" to describe these culturally created and often unstable systems. Historians interested in gender asserted that it was an appropriate category of analysis when looking at *all* historical developments, not simply those involving women or the family. *Every* political, intellectual, religious, economic, social, and even military change impacted the actions and roles of men and women, and, conversely, a culture's gender structures influenced every other structure or development. People's notions of gender shaped not only the way they thought about men and women, but also the way they thought about their society in general. As the historian Joan Scott put it in an extremely influential 1986 article in the *American Historical Review*, "Gender is a constitutive element of social relationships based on perceived differences between the sexes, and gender is a primary way of signifying relationships of power."[5] Thus hierarchies in other realms of life were often expressed in terms of gender, with dominant individuals or groups described in masculine terms and dependent ones in feminine. These ideas in turn affected the way people acted, though explicit and symbolic ideas of gender could also conflict with the way men and women chose or were forced to operate in the world.

Gender swept academia, and then ordinary speech. Scholars in many fields increasingly switched from "sex" to "gender" as the acceptable terminology: "Sex roles" became "gender roles," "sex distinctions" became "gender distinctions," and so on, and several university presses started book series with "gender" in their titles. Most of the studies with "gender" in the title still focused on women—and women's history continued as its own field—but a few looked equally at both sexes or concentrated on the male experience, calling their work "men's history" or the "new men's studies." Courses created in or after the 1980s tended to use "gender" instead of "women" in their titles, or sometimes both, and included consideration of masculinity, fatherhood, and other issues related to men. As scholars associated with gay and lesbian studies increasingly emphasized the distinction between gender and sexuality, their courses came to be titled "sexuality and gender," or something similar. Many programs and centers also changed their titles, to "Gender Studies," "Women's and Gender Studies," or "Women, Gender and Sexuality Studies," although some did not, as they viewed doing so as a watering down of the political thrust of women's studies or a downplaying of its connections with the feminist movement.

Name changes in programs were sometimes controversial, and the insight that gender is an appropriate category of analysis when looking at every historical development was both controversial and hard to implement in courses. Gender was easier to include as a topic than as a perspective. As the personnel of history departments gradually came to include more people who had encountered gender in their own training, gender (along with race and class) came to feature more prominently in general history courses, but there was also resistance on the part of faculty and students. Student evaluations of instructors who discussed gender inevitably included complaints: Why did you talk so much about women? This course was supposed to be about the Renaissance (or colonial America, or modern China, or whatever). Some saw this as part of a feminist or liberal plot. Along with resistance, there was lethargy, lack of time to revise courses, and the ubiquitous problem of coverage: What do I take out when I add something new?

Coverage was a particular issue in the world history courses that were becoming a common part of departmental arrays in some universities in the 1970s and 1980s, as these surveyed vast sweeps of geography as well as long units of time. In the United States, history that moved beyond a national focus grew out of area studies programs and individual or university initiatives and was usually labeled "world history," while in Britain, Canada, Australia, and continental Europe diplomatic history widened into imperial, international, and "overseas" history. Like women's history, these subfields had their own debates and controversies about conceptualizations, inclusion, and scope. Courses often began as ones on various "civilizations" around the world considered separately, which tended to promote a binary model of "the West and the rest," with an overemphasis on the West that in the 1980s came to be labeled "Eurocentrism." Gradually many of those teaching world history rejected that model in favor of one that emphasized connections, interactions, and multipronged comparisons. Courses and research in world, imperial, and international history tended to focus on political economy and large-scale political and economic processes carried out by governments and commercial elites. This provided fewer easy links for issues of gender than did social history, so there was little intersection between world and international history and women's/gender history at this point.

Women's/gender history and world/international history were confronted by similar challenges to their approaches and assumptions in the 1980s and 1990s. Prime among these was the assertion that because historical sources always present a biased and partial picture and historians themselves have particular perspectives and motivations, to suggest that one can fully determine what happened or why is foolish or misguided.[6] What historians should do instead is to analyze discourse—the written and visual materials of the past—to determine the way various things are represented in them and their possible meanings. This heightened interest in discourse among historians, usually labeled the "linguistic turn" or the "cultural turn," drew on the ideas of literary and linguistic theory—often loosely termed "deconstruction" or "poststructuralism" or "postmodernism"—about the power of language and the indeterminacy of truth. Language is so powerful, argued some theorists, that it determines, rather than simply describes, our understanding of the world; knowledge is passed down through language, and knowledge is power. Texts as well as events have unstable meanings, argued many, so that seeking out the intent of an author is also silly. "The author is dead" became a catchphrase, and literary scholars instead studied texts themselves and their varied and changing reception.

This emphasis on the relationship of knowledge to power, and on the power of language, made poststructuralism attractive to feminist scholars in many disciplines, who themselves already emphasized the ways language and other structures of knowledge excluded women. The insight of the French philosopher Michel Foucault that the body is central to political economies and that power comes from everywhere fit with the feminist recognition that "the personal is political" and that misogyny and other forces that limited women's lives could be found in many places: in fashion magazines, fairy tales, and jokes told at work as well as overt job discrimination and domestic violence. Many postcolonial scholars were also postmodern, emphasizing the language of hierarchy and domination, and noting that subordinated groups often developed their own distinctive and more liberating meanings for such language. Historians of gender and sexuality in various parts of the world were thus prominent exponents of the linguistic turn, and many analyzed representations of women, men, the body, sexual actions, and related topics in their research, and focused on these in their classes. Some wondered whether it made sense to talk about "women" or "men" at all, because people's experiences differed so much based on their class, race, nationality, ethnicity, religion, and other factors. If, for example, women were thought to be delicate guardians of the home, as was true in the nineteenth-century United States, then were black women, who worked in fields alongside men, really women? If an essential part of masculinity was heading a household and fathering chil-

dren, then were eunuch soldiers in medieval Byzantium or China or celi-
bate priests in medieval Europe really men? Were "woman" and "man"
valid categories whose meaning is self-evident and unchanging over time,
or is arguing for any biological base for gender difference naive "essentialism" and an attempt to impose a dichotomy on what was a much more
complex situation?[7] Gender was performative, some argued, that is, a role
that was developed through repetition; it was something one *did* rather
than something one *was*.[8]

Biology actually provided evidence to support these doubts, as no physical indicator of sex difference—external and internal genitalia, chromo-
somes, hormones—has proven to be absolutely dichotomous, and there
are intersexed individuals of many varieties.[9] Even those whose sexual and
reproductive organs and chromosomal and hormonal patterns mark them
as male or female may mentally regard themselves as the other, or they
may understand themselves as "transgendered," that is, as neither male nor
female or both male and female or as being in the wrong body for their assigned sex.[10] Cultural ethnography and world history provided evidence as
well, for in a number of areas throughout the world, there were and are individuals who temporarily or permanently were categorized or understood
themselves to be neither male nor female.[11] A dichotomous gender system,
and perhaps even gender itself, might be a colonizing category of analysis
just as race was, argued some postcolonial scholars. Such evidence indicated to many that gender is indeed performative, and some instructors
teaching gender history began to include discussion of intersexed individuals and third gender categories, although never talking about women or
men, or always putting these in quotation marks, proved too cumbersome
to be a consistent practice.

The wide variations across cultures and across time in everything related to sexuality indicated to many that sexuality was primarily a matter of social construction and performance as well, and that attempts to
find a basis for sexual orientation in the body were futile or ill-advised. In
the 1990s, a period of intense HIV-AIDS activism, scholars combined elements of gay and lesbian studies with other concepts originating in literary and feminist analysis to develop queer theory. Queer theorists argued

that, like gender, sexual notions were central to all aspects of culture, and they called for greater attention to sexuality that was at odds with whatever was defined as "normal" or that blurred categories. In the last decade, queer theory has been widely applied, as scholars have "queered"—that is, called into question the categories used to describe and analyze—the nation, race, religion, time, and other topics along with gender and sexuality. This broadening has led some—including a few of the founders of the field—to wonder whether queer theory loses its punch when everything is queer, but it continues to be an influential theoretical perspective, and courses in queer theory are a staple in cultural studies and women's and gender studies programs.[12]

While many historians embraced the linguistic/cultural turn, its emphasis on discourse and representation elicited harsh responses from others, including many who focused on women, gender, and sexuality or on areas of the world outside the West. They asserted that it denied people the ability to shape their world—what is usually termed "agency"—in both past and present by positing unchangeable linguistic structures. Was it not ironic, they noted, that just as women and gay people and indigenous groups were asserting they were *part* of history, "history" became just a text? And that just as women and people outside the Western literary tradition were coming into critical visibility as writers, the author was pronounced dead? They wondered whether the idea that gender, sexuality, race, and other categories were simply unstable historical or social constructs denied the very real oppression that many in the past (and present) experienced and was thus a turning away from engaged scholarship. Cultural historians, and cultural studies scholars more generally, argued that this was not so, but that their field *was* politically engaged because it critically examined the dynamics and cultural practices of power. Disagreements were sharp and sometimes personal, but by the 2000s, that debate seemed to have run its course. As the cultural historian Lynn Hunt has recently commented, "Most historians have simply moved on, incorporating insights from postmodern positions but not feeling obliged to take a stand on its epistemological claims."[13]

Along with the linguistic turn and the rise of cultural studies, the 1990s also brought other new directions in history at larger scales, including transnational history, big history, the history of globalization, and global history. Although some scholars distinguish between world and global history, their definitions of each are idiosyncratic and sometimes contradictory, and there is far more overlap than difference, which is why this primer puts them together. Both have been overwhelmingly Anglophone and, given the scholarly diaspora, disproportionally institutionally situated in the United States and the United Kingdom. Thus many scholars in other parts of the world have rejected world and global history as hopelessly Eurocentric intellectual neocolonialism, yet another tool for rule and domination. Some have instead focused intently on movements and migrations, creating diasporic and connected histories that do not call themselves "world" or "global." Others have posited different centers, creating Afrocentric and Sinocentric world histories. But others have called for a more polycentric world history and are building on different national and regional roots and traditions to create this multivocal version, working upward and outward from the available sources in multiple languages and from multiple sites.[14]

Such multivocality is also a feature of gender and sexuality, as even the categories that had developed through challenges to the standard gender and sexual dichotomies became categories of gender and sexual identity themselves: LGBTTQQI2S (lesbian, gay, bisexual, transsexual, transgender, queer, questioning, intersexed, two-spirit). Both activists and theorists wondered whether this separation into categories was politically useful or even valid, because it negated the key insight that these categories were (and are) constructed, artificial, and changing. Some celebrated efforts at blurring or bending categories, viewing any sort of identity as both false and oppressive and celebrating hybridity and performance. The concept of intersectionality, with its insistence that gender should not be considered apart from other identities but is always materialized in terms of and by means of them, provided support for this point of view, and people now describe themselves on their blogs, Facebook pages, and Twitter or Tumblr posts as "intersectional feminists." The phrase was so common in the women's marches held around the world on January 21, 2017, that many newspapers, magazines, and websites felt the need to explain it. But identity politics are here to stay, and so are gender and sexual categories, shifting and problematic as they are. And women's/gender/sexuality history continues to have a political thrust. People within the gay rights and transgender movements in many parts of the world today, for example, use historical third and trans gender categories to demonstrate the variety in indigenous understandings of gender and sexuality and to stress that demands for rights for homosexuals or trans people are not simply a Western import. To put this in the high-theory speak of Spivak, they "engage in a strategic use of positivist essentialism in a scrupulously visible political interest."[15] Courses in the history of transsexual and transgender people are beginning to be offered, or units inserted into existing courses, as "add and stir" takes a new form.

All these scholarly turns over the last fifty years should help shape your answer to "why teach the history of women, gender, and sexuality?" and make your statement of course goals more complex than it would have been decades ago. Here is one possibility:

> In this course, students will examine world historical patterns and processes, with a focus on issues concerning women, gender, and sexuality. They will come to understand how gender and sexuality have been socially and culturally constructed by global historical developments into highly variable and historically changing systems of power relations, and have in turn shaped other events and structures. They will evaluate how gender and sexuality intersect with other forms of identity and systems of power such as class, race, and ethnicity, and how and why the ideas and actions of individuals and groups, as well as cross-cultural interactions, have transformed these over time. Using primary sources that present a variety of perspectives, along with secondary materials, students will develop credible and effective narratives and analyses about gender and sexuality in the past that show understanding of the contexts of different historical eras and cultures.

You may notice several things about this statement of learning goals. First, even though it incorporates ideas that come from various scholarly turns, it does not contain certain terms that have been central parts of these, such as performativity, agency, essentialism, and discourse. That is intentional. The audience for this statement is primarily the student deciding whether or not to take or stay in your course, and including scholarly jargon is not an effective sales pitch. In fact, depending on where you teach and the level of the course, the statement as written might be pitched too high, and you should adjust it to better match your students, along with adding or subtracting things depending on your own aims, or just writing your own.[16] (A secondary audience might be administrators or committees who oversee syllabi, which could shape the form this needs to take or wording that has to be there. Fitting what you actually want to do in the course into the prescribed format might take some juggling, but it is usually not difficult.)

Second, the statement does not include social transformation or political change as one of the course goals. That is also intentional. The histories of women, gender, and sexuality have always been accused of "having an agenda," and they do. Helping students understand that gender and sexuality are socially constructed and historically changing and that these are systems of power that people have transformed is a pretty forceful agenda. Investigating gender in the past is a political act, an assertion that the story we have been told is not only incomplete (all history is, of course, incomplete) but to some degree intentionally incomplete, as sources, actions, and sometimes people themselves were forgotten and suppressed. But historians have an agenda in everything they teach. Even statements as seemingly innocuous as the AHA History Discipline Core's assertion that students should have "empathy for historical actors" and "respect for interpretive debate" and should "develop positions that reflect deliberation, cooperation, and diverse perspectives" reflect an agenda, and one that is not uncontested. You may want to make learning to challenge as well as understand oppressive power relations one of your course goals, or to highlight the feminist nature of your pedagogy by noting your classroom culture will be collaborative and democratic. Whether these objectives are implicit or explicit is up to you; your course goals should be your own, as much as the power structure in which you and your course are enmeshed will allow.

Choosing a Focus and a Title

WOMEN, GENDER, OR SEXUALITY?

OUR SECOND DESIGN PRINCIPLE, directly related to your purpose in teaching the course, is *choosing a focus*. This should be reflected in the course title and any description that you prepare. These should honestly reflect your course, but pay some attention to how students might react, as the best course is pointless if no one enrolls. Course titles and official descriptions are often cumbersome to change, so create yours carefully.

Do you want your students primarily to learn about women's experiences, and so to examine the female life cycle, ideas about women, women's work, women's sexuality, and women writers and artists? Then your focus should be on women, and the word "women" should probably appear in your course title. This does not mean the course needs to be structured around women's accomplishments and contributions—what Natalie Davis has called the "women worthies" approach—as courses did in the past. Nor do you need to present a totalizing or uniform story of women's status rising and falling (for which the standard version is up among the gatherer/hunters of the Paleolithic, down in the classical period, including the Vedic era in South Asia and ancient Athens, up with the end of the classical empires, especially among the nomadic Mongols and tribal societies, down in the Song dynasty in China and in the Italian Renaissance, further down with colonization and the slave trade, up in the women's rights movements and the wars of the twentieth century, down in subsequent eras of backlash and in neoliberalism). Instead your course can build on the critiques and refinements of earlier approaches to women's history and examine not only commonalities but also differences among women along many lines—race, class, nationality, religion, ability, sexual orientation, and so on.[1] Thus a course that focuses on women can reflect the insight that systems of hierarchy and oppression are interlocking and intersectional. "Women" is, after all, a plural noun.

There are several two-volume works that you could use as the basic textbook for the class, although these tend to present areas of the world separately in a somewhat older approach, so you would need to highlight connections and comparisons.[2] The Roy Rosenzweig Center for History and New Media (CHNM) at George Mason University has a fantastic website, *Women in World History*, with primary sources (some grouped in thematic modules) and long introductions contextualizing these, teaching strategies, discussion questions, website reviews, and other materials.[3] You could actually teach a very good course using only the materials on this website, and your students would pay nothing!

Do you want your students primarily to learn about the social and cultural construction of gender and how this changed across time, that is, about ideas, norms, laws, depictions, and practices concerning women, men, and genders beyond the primary two? Then your course should focus on gender and have "gender" in the title. This does not mean that you have to limit your course to discourse and representation, however, or to reject agency and emphasize the power of unchangeable linguistic structures. We have moved, as even key practitioners of cultural history have noted, beyond the cultural turn, but can use its insights about meaning and multiple interpretations as we examine things other than texts, such as the people who wrote them and the developments that spawned or resulted from them. So you can teach a course about gender and still talk about causation.[4] In fact, to really capture the revolutionary potential of gender analysis, you can explore the way that gender causes or at least shapes developments in every aspect of life—political, intellectual, religious, economic, social, and even military—as well as the more common focus on the other line of causation. Thus along with discussing, say, the impact of Christianity on gender norms and structures in the Roman Empire, you can talk about how Roman notions of gender shaped both Christianity and the empire; or alongside examining how the Communist Revolution shaped ideas about masculinity and femininity in China, you can examine the impact of changing gender ideals on the formation and evolution of the People's Republic.[5] Peter Stearns's *Gender in World History* and my (Merry's) *Gender in History: Global Perspectives* (discussed in chapter 3) are both relatively brief overviews that could be combined with other materials, including the CHNM websites.[6]

Do you want your students primarily to learn about sexuality, or about same-sex attraction, or about sexuality that was not the norm (however that was defined)? Then your course title should include "sexuality," "homosexuality," "LGBTQ," "queer," or some other term, with your choice among these made to best reflect what you actually plan to do. As with women's history, this does not mean that the course will be "Great Gays of the Past" the way it might have been forty years ago, and as with gender history, it does not mean that you focus only on social construction, the way you might have thirty years ago. As you historicize sexuality, you will probably discuss the idea, derived from Michel Foucault's *History of Sexuality*, that sexual orientation and perhaps even sexuality itself are concepts that were created fairly recently (meaning sometime between the seventeenth century and the nineteenth century), as part of what is usually labeled the development of "modern sexuality." Before this point there were sexual acts, but only after this did people come to think they had a sexual orientation that was part of their identity. This conceptual insight sparked much research, but also criticism, which you can now integrate into your course as well. Queer theory, for example, has challenged the acts versus identities, modern versus premodern binary—what Eve Kosofsky Sedgwick has satirically termed the "Great Paradigm Shift"—as overly dichotomizing and unreflective of the performative nature of all categories.[7] And scholars who focus on areas outside the West have noted that the notion of sexual "modernity" tends to make the United States and Europe appear "progressive" while other parts of the world are "traditional" or "oppressive" rather than just different.[8] But other historians have built on Foucault's idea rather than rejecting it. Susan Lanser, for example, has emphasized the role of sexuality as a causative agent in the creation of modernity, as ideas about sexual relations stimulated broader debates about power, liberty, order, and difference, making sexuality "not only an effect but a stimulus."[9]

In terms of materials for the classroom, Peter Stearns again has a brief survey, *Sexuality in World History*, and if you want to focus on the modern period, there is a collection edited by Robert M. Buffington, Eithne Luibhéid, and Donna J. Guy, *A Global History of Sexuality: The Modern Period* (both discussed in chapter 3). There is no teaching-focused website with original sources only on sexuality (though the CHNM websites have some), but Matthew Kuefler's *The History of Sexuality Sourcebook* includes a wide-ranging collection of nearly two hundred sources from antiquity to the present, with good headnotes.[10]

Do you want your students to learn about all of these? Then design a course that includes all three, but we think it is still important to make distinctions among them and to explain that these are overlapping fields of study, but not the same. Women are not the only ones with gender, just as men are not the only ones with class. This distinction is similar to that made successfully some years ago, when the "add women and stir" approach had resulted in sections labeled "women and the family" in many textbooks and general introductory courses. Yes, women's lives were often more shaped by family structures than were those of men, asserted historians of women, but they were not *only* shaped by these, and men's lives were shaped by their families far more than was often recognized. Women's history and family history were separate, though complementary, fields.

Whether you choose women, gender, sexuality, or some combination of these, you can design a course that reflects insights drawn from all three: You can approach topics intersectionally and with an emphasis on multivocality and diversity; you can use gender as a lens to examine any topic (including sexuality); you can queer anything—that is, call into question the categories used to describe and analyze things, especially if these are dichotomous. How you will do all this in a ten-week quarter or a fifteen-week semester is another issue, but deciding what to leave out is the hardest part of designing any course in history, especially those in world or global history.

You can also incorporate insights from all three into your general world history classes, of course, using gender and sexuality as perspectives as well as subjects. Ulrike Strasser and Heidi Tinsman provide excellent guidance for how they did this in a team-taught large survey course at the University of California–Irvine, "World History: Gender and Politics, 1400–1789," in which they "ask students to consider how gender and sexuality centrally constitute relations of power within, across, and between societies, [and] be attentive to the ways in which historical actors subvert and resist dominant norms of gender and sexuality and thus challenge the authorities representing these norms."[11] The same two authors reflect on ways that the successful integration of masculinity into narratives of the changing political economy in Latin America—in the expansion of the Aztec, Inca, and Spanish empires; the close link between nation building and the promotion of male-headed families in the nineteenth century; and transformations in labor systems—can serve as a model for how to do the same in general world history courses.[12]

Similarly, Trevor Getz and Liz Clarke's award-winning graphic history *Abina and the Important Men*, based on an 1876 court transcript of a West African woman who was wrongfully enslaved, escaped, and then took her former master to court, provides suggestions for how to use the book to teach gender and sexuality as well as slavery, colonialism, and Africa in the world history classroom. In its second edition, along with the striking visual narrative, historical contextualization, and reading guide that were in the first edition, it includes a longer discussion of gender and the complex relationship between slavery and marriage in African society. To this are added reflections on these issues from several leading historians, making the book—and the app that goes with it—an excellent choice for specialized courses on women and gender in world history as well as general surveys.[13]

Whether in a course specifically focusing on women, gender, and/or sexuality or in a more general world history course, including reproduction and its demographic consequences as a theme can provide a good way to link gender and sexuality with other topics as well as connect your course to contemporary issues. After 1750, global population began to go up at a steadily increasing rate because of a decline in death rates due to a more stable food supply, better transport networks, and public health measures. Population zoomed. Birth rates in industrialized countries began to go down slightly in the first half of the twentieth century, and more substantially in the 1960s with new methods of birth control including the pill and the intra-uterine device, combined with greater cultural acceptance of contraception and in some places, such as China and Puerto Rico, government policies promoting small families. Today the world's lowest fertility rates are in the wealthy, heavily urbanized, and crowded states of East Asia, including Singapore, Hong Kong, Macao, and Japan, where birth rates are so low that the population is declining, and in Eastern Europe and the former Soviet states, where what sociologists term "partner instability" and other uncertainties have led women to decide not to have children. Fertility rates remain high in the world's poorest countries, however, and among rural populations in many developing countries. In India, for example, middle-class urban families have access to contraception and thus have smaller families, while families in villages remain large; demographers predict that as of 2050 India will pass China as the world's most populous country, with 1.5 billion people. These demographic trends are often presented in a nongendered and sometimes dehumanized way, as charts and graphs, but underlying them are norms about gender and sexuality as well as political and economic relationships of power. Population growth has been reduced in some quite poor countries through strict government policies or subsidized contraception, for example, but international aid programs have also been hampered in this by stringent limitations on the types of birth control they are allowed to provide that result from the moral and religious concerns of political pressure groups within wealthier countries. Any course in world history of the twentieth and twenty-first centuries has to talk about the impact of a rising global population, and it will help your students better connect with this issue if you present this in human terms rather than simply as numbers.

In terms of specific courses, whatever you decide about your focus, it is best to be as honest as possible. If you focus on women, do not use "gender" in the course name, and if you focus only on LGBTQ issues, do not title it "sexuality." You should also be honest about the geographic and chronological parameters of your course. If you want to focus on sexuality in the West, say that is what you are doing, and tell students up front about *when* as well as *where*: "The history of sexuality in the West from X to Y." (And see chapter 3 about why you need to explain to your students why you chose X and Y.) Or if your course is really about sexuality in the United States, do not title it "The History of Sexuality." Michel Foucault could get away with this sweeping title in 1976 for a book about two centuries in Europe, but we cannot do so today, and he actually envisioned his work as an eventual seven volumes that would have had a long chronological sweep. One of the great insights of gender and race theory is that of marked and unmarked categories (artists and women artists, writers and black writers), and it is good to model this right up front in your course title.

If you use the word "world" or "global" in your title, make sure that your course is geographically balanced, and not marked by the "West and the Rest" conceptualization that was common earlier in the teaching of world history. Whether in general courses or those focusing on women, gender, and sexuality, the proper balance in world history courses is not half Europe or the United States and half everything else, nor should Europe or the United States be one pole of every comparison. Thus instead of comparing women's rights movements in the United States and France, try France and Japan, or Japan and India.[14] Or if you are discussing same-sex sociability, compare lesbian bars and clubs in Berlin and Shanghai.[15] When you are deciding what to leave out, try leaving out the U.S. or European example; there is a chance that students might already know something about this anyway, and an even better chance they will never have heard of the examples you choose for the topic you are talking about from somewhere else in the world. But do not leave the United States out completely, as that reinforces the notion of American exceptionalism; despite efforts to deny it, the United States is part of the world. Your discussion of the gendered impact of globalization in the late twentieth and early twenty-first centuries, for example, can link the decline of older industrial centers in the United States and Britain with largely male workforces into "Rust Belts" of aging machines to the opening of giant factories with largely female workforces in China, Bangladesh, Vietnam, Puerto Rico, Mexico, and wherever else wages were low. The actual feminization of manufacturing work and the dramatic boom-and-bust cycles of globalized industries have led men's work in many areas to also become "feminized," that is, lower waged and not bound by long-term contracts or providing much job security or benefits such as pensions. Nostalgia for older labor patterns and gender norms, combined with worries about globalization and migration, fueled right-wing populist and nationalist movements in the early twenty-first century, a development in which you can help your students connect the local and the global.

We have couched the preceding discussion in terms of "as much as possible" because even if you are designing a completely new course, it generally has to fit within the existing structure of a history department or an interdisciplinary women's and gender studies program (or both). It also often has to be approved by a departmental, divisional, and sometimes university-wide committee and follow guidelines about what needs to be stated on the syllabus about policies and assessment. If you want your course to count for distributional or general education requirements, or to cross-list with other programs, there are often still more rules. All of these may shape what you can title your course or how you can describe its content, and increasingly these may also determine certain aspects of your syllabus, such as your delineation of course learning goals or requirements. Sometimes the parameters set by committees or as centrally mandated obligations seem silly, and if they have been influenced by political forces they may be worse than that. But most schema of learning goals are fairly broad and vague, with "critical thinking," "understanding diversity," "effective communication of ideas," and similar phrases among them, so you should be able to fit your own course goals and assignments within them. Besides, as those of us who have been teaching a long time know well, students rarely read the whole syllabus anyway, and they certainly skip over any standardized polysyllabic mumbo-jumbo that they see on every syllabus, so they will not pay attention to it on yours. What they will want to know is how many books they have to buy and what they have to do to get a high grade.

Designing any course involves considering how it will fit into a system of requirements so that students will actually take it, but courses on women, gender, and/or sexuality in any discipline face other issues in terms of student appeal. Although we advocate truth in advertising, certain course titles will result in fewer students in the room, and thus fewer students who will gain what you want them to from the course. For example, at the University of Wisconsin–Milwaukee, the title of the freshman-level course in what is basically gender history is "Family and Sex Roles in the Past," a title that has not changed since it was first offered in 1980. The title uses an out-of-date formulation—"sex roles" rather than "gender roles"—and links this with the family, another older approach. But ever since it was first offered, this course has filled to capacity and attracted students more balanced in terms of gender than do courses titled "women's history," so the title has stayed, though the course is now very different than it was originally. The same is true with course titles elsewhere: "Sex" draws best, "gender" draws better than "women," and "feminism" is an enrollment killer. In this era when student enrollment numbers are closely scrutinized by college and university officials and often determine departmental resources (or even salaries), this is not something that can be taken lightly. So you could develop a catchy title for your course that is still true to its content: "War, Wealth, and Witches: Gender in the Early Modern World"; "Veiling Madonnas, Creating Martyrs: Women and Power in World History"; "Doing Gender Globally: Global Sexualities, Past and Present."

Titling your course in a specific way, and fitting it into a system of requirements in a certain way, will influence the *types* of students you draw as well as their total numbers, which may (and actually should) in turn shape the way you structure the course and what you expect students to do. In history departments, courses on women, gender, and/or sexuality generally parallel other thematic and topical courses that have been developed as departments have tried to figure out what to add to their still largely nation-ally and regionally based courses to globalize their curricula and respond to changing student interests and changes in history as a field. Sometimes these are lower-level courses, and sometimes they are upper-level. If your course is a lower-level one, the students may be taking it to fulfill general education requirements and have taken no other university-level history. If your course is an upper-level one, some proportion of your students will be history majors, and you can expect them to have had at least a few courses in history, although not necessarily anything with a global perspective, as requirements for history majors generally have a less rigid progression than do those for other majors. Students taking your course through women's and gender studies or LGBTQ programs may have some familiarity with core concepts related to gender and sexuality, but not necessarily any his-tory. Course reading and assignments will need to take these factors into account, and what this means in practical terms is that you often have to do a quick run through basic geography and history at the start of every unit. Maps are invaluable.

Wherever your course is institutionally located, and despite all you have done to make its title and description broadly appealing, your students will be self-selecting, for even if it fulfills requirements, almost nowhere will your specific course be required. If the word "women" is in the title, it will primarily attract women (and a few brave men whose mothers are feminists or who are taking the course with their girlfriends). If the word "sexuality" is in the title, it will attract LGBTQ students. Whatever it is titled, the students will not only be interested in women's, gender, LGBTQ, and/or trans issues (or at least not threatened by these), but many of them will also be politically and personally committed. This will make it different from most other courses in history, and make teaching it both more challenging and more rewarding.

Chapter Three

Organizing Material

CHRONOLOGICAL AND THEMATIC APPROACHES

ONCE YOU HAVE decided why you want to teach your course, and what you want your primary focus to be, you will need to consider *organizing your material*, our third design principle. Dividing the whole course by region generally leads to a fair amount of repetition, and presents an old-fashioned view of world history, as newer approaches have deemphasized individual cultures and civilizations and instead highlighted movements and flows across borders, entangled and shared histories, and hybridity. Thus though regional comparisons are fine, we would not recommend a regional organization. A thematic organization can work, and we discuss this at the end of the chapter. Because most history courses are organized chronologically to highlight change over time, we spend most of the chapter on ways to do this.

Periodization is contested in women's and gender history and also in world history. Focusing on women has often disrupted existing chronological categories, especially those that carried implicit (or explicit) value judgments. The Renaissance and the Enlightenment lost some of their luster once women were part of the story, as did the democracy of ancient Athens or Jacksonian America. In world history, the developments that historians have seen as marking a division between one period and the next occurred at widely varying times around the world, making it difficult to avoid the notion that some places were "advanced" while others were "backward." And bringing global and gendered approaches together creates further issues: Histories of sexuality, for example, often use the division between "premodern" and "modern" as an organizing principle, but this break has been contested, especially by those who focus on areas outside the West. So your organization might involve a bit looser chronology than that of courses that focus on political history, for which wars and revolutions provide handy break points. Here we provide several options and discuss some books designed for classroom use that fit with many of these.

You could start in the Paleolithic, reflecting the expanded time frame increasingly common in world history, in which the development of writing is no longer seen as a sharp break between "history" and "prehistory." Starting with the Paleolithic means you will pay attention to what the material record can reveal about gender, which could become one of the themes that you follow throughout the course. Material culture studies is a robust field today, with roots in art history, archaeology, anthropology, and history, and it poses questions about the role of objects and the relationships between things and people in the creation and transformation of society and culture. A focus on material culture works very well in women's and gender history, allowing your students to examine aspects of life that have been produced, consumed, and given meaning by women as well as men, including food, clothing, household goods, and ritual objects.

Mary Jo Maynes and Ann Waltner's *The Family: A World History*, a book that examines "how world history looks when the family is the center of the story" and that grew out of the authors co-teaching a course on the history of the family at the University of Minnesota, offers one chronology for a course starting in the distant past.[1] Although women and the family are not the same topic (a point emphasized by both women's and family historians), a chronology based on the history of families could work quite well for a course that focuses on women or gender. The material is organized into seven chapters, each covering a specified chronological period: domestic life and human origins (to 5000 BCE); family in the emergence of religions (to 1000 CE); ruling families and kinship at the dawn of politics (ca. 3000 BCE to 1450 CE); early modern families (1400–1750); families in global markets (1600–1850); families in revolutionary times (1750–1920); and families in the era of state population management (1880 to the present). You will notice that the chronologies overlap, and that most chapters also have a specific topical or thematic focus, including religion and the family, ruling families, and families and global trade. This combination of chronological and topical organization is quite common in world history courses, where certain themes emerge as more significant in some eras than others.

Speaking practically, dividing your course into the seven periods set out in the book would give you roughly two weeks per period in a fifteen-week semester, meaningful chunks for your students. Within each period, you could begin with general points, and then focus on several areas of the world or social groups, with comparisons among them. These more detailed discussions should include some topics that are standards in world history, such as Confucianism in China or the industrial revolution in England, both because these are important to the history of gender and because doing so reinforces the point that what you are teaching is not off in some separate sphere, unconnected to "real" history. They can also include more unusual subjects, however. Discussed in the book, for example, is the complex relationship among family, ethnic categories, and citizenship in nineteenth-century Algeria, where French colonial authorities enlisted European women in the program of spreading French culture, language, and family norms, with an eye to eventually making some colonial subjects "French enough" to become citizens. The French "civilizing mission" relied in part on claims that Muslim culture kept women subservient, but the French women active in this were not men's legal equals themselves. (France did not allow women to vote until 1945, and even after that many legal disparities continued.)

For each of your topics, we would recommend highlighting a specific individual or two, which brings the story down from the level of generalization and gives people agency. Again using the book as an example, the section on Algeria describes Isabelle Eberhardt, a young European woman who after moving to Algeria with her mother adopted male Bedouin dress so that she could move more freely, thus becoming more Algerian instead of trying to make Algerians more French. These specific examples provide a great opportunity to include people and stories from your own research, which you can use as evidence for more general developments. Do not worry that these represent only one variation on a theme; that is true with everything in world history, and one or two well-chosen examples make any development more meaningful than trying to cover the whole world every time. World historians emphasize that variations in both chronological and geographic scale are important tools of understanding, and your course can incorporate this insight.

Peter Stearns's *Sexuality in World History* provides a similar seven-part chronological framework, beginning in the Paleolithic, easily adaptable to a course on sexuality or in which sexuality is a key theme.[2] There are four chapters in a first section titled "Sexuality before Modern Times": sexuality and the rise of agriculture (100,000 BCE–2000 BCE); sexuality in the classical period (1000 BCE–500 CE); the impact of religion on sexuality to 1450; and sex in an age of trade and colonies (1450–1750). There are two chapters in a second section titled "Sex in the Modern World": a first sexual revolution and the Victorian response in Western society from 1750 to 1950; then global trends and variations in the age of imperialism (1750–1950). And there is one chapter in a third section titled "Sexuality in the Age of Globalization": sex in contemporary world history (1950–present). As with Maynes and Waltner's *The Family*, the story begins with foraging societies in the Paleolithic, religion is a particular point of focus across a broad sweep of the premodern period, and other periods are also connected with specific topics. Using this chronological organization would again give you seven two-week periods in a semester, and connect with major themes in world history, including the domestication of plants and animals (which is itself about sex, though we do not often discuss it that way) and imperialism.

Given the focus on sexuality in Stearns's book, there is a distinct division between the premodern and the modern, with the break at about 1750. Stearns notes the disputes surrounding the idea that "modern sexuality" began at a specific point, because this schema ignores great variations between societies and downplays the continuing force of traditional attitudes. He still views the middle of the eighteenth century as the beginning of a change in sexual behavior and values, however, as sexual activity (and childbirth) outside marriage increased, doctors began to claim authority over sexual matters, and sexual pleasure was discussed more openly in pornography and other sorts of literature. The year 1750 is a very common dividing line in world history, usually seen as the beginning of the "age of revolution," with discussions of the American, French, and Haitian revolutions. Thus suggesting the possibility that there was also, to use Stearns's phrase, a first "sexual revolution" at this point allows you to note the way social and political changes interwove. Even if you end up emphasizing continuities more than change across this line, you have encouraged students to think about why it was so much easier to end a system of government that had lasted for centuries and lop off a king's head than to upend sexual mores, so have made the point about how deeply embedded gender and sexual norms are in a culture.

Stearns sees the 1950s as another break, because of the birth control pill, legal changes that allowed greater sexual openness in the media, the "sexual revolution," the rise of global consumerized sex, and the beginnings of conservative reactions to all this. The history of contraception is a topic your students will rarely have learned about in secondary school as it is too controversial to make it into most textbooks, but it is one that grabs their attention. You can thread this and other issues surrounding reproduction throughout your course, noting efforts to both encourage reproduction (herbs, charms, rituals, special foods, certain sexual positions, aphrodisiacs, prayer, and so on) and discourage it (dung pessaries, herbs, condoms, vigorous activity, avoiding certain times of the month, sterilization, as well as modern chemical, mechanical, and surgical methods). Who controls reproduction and to what ends are questions that can allow you to weave in issues of power and hierarchy, from the level of the household to the empire.

Some of you may be uncomfortable with a course that covers such a long sweep of time, worried about being superficial as you race through the millennia, or you may be really eager to get to the twentieth or even the twenty-first century. Then start your course at some point more recent than the Paleolithic. You could begin with the invention of writing, for example, not because this marked the beginning of "history," but because it marked the beginning of a system in which access to many types of knowledge was more open to men than to women of the same social group. Until the twentieth century far fewer women were taught to read and write than men, and gender disparities in literacy continue; the UNESCO Institute for Statistics reported in 2014 that two-thirds of the adults around the world who cannot read or write are women. Thus from its invention to now, writing has been gendered. Writing also meant that gender distinctions were more formalized, for among the earliest of the world's written records, whether in Mesopotamia, Egypt, China, or elsewhere, were laws specifying how husbands and wives were to treat each other, religious literature setting out the proper conduct for men and women, and stories and myths that described relations between men and women, or gods and goddesses. *Sharing the World Stage: Biography and Gender in World History* begins with a chapter on King Hammurabi of Babylon (r. 1792–1750 BCE), which includes many provisions from his famous law code that regulate marriage, divorce, inheritance, and other matters.[3] It also includes letters written on clay cuneiform tablets from and to the much-less-well-known Queen Sibtu of Mari (a city-state north of Babylon), Hammurabi's contemporary, who looked after affairs of state and directed the labor force of the palace when her husband, King Zimri-Lin, was away. The book continues with paired biographies of men and women and groups of relevant original sources through sixteen largely chronologically arranged chapters within two volumes. Hammurabi's code would work well as a starting point for your course, as long as you make clear that we have no way of knowing the extent to which these and other early laws were enforced, as records of actual court proceedings do not begin to survive until thousands of years later, and then only rarely. Laws and other prescriptive statements were not the same as lived experience. That distinction between theory and practice could provide a theme to follow throughout the course, in fact, as selective enforcement of laws lies behind some of today's most important political and social protest movements.

You could begin in the classical period, with the more formal considerations of the nature of women and men, and speculations—couched in the language of religion, medicine, or philosophy—about reasons for the differences between them. Many of the educated men who were the primary authors of recorded cultural traditions thought and wrote about women, trying to determine what makes them different from men, whom they regarded as the unmarked or default category in terms of gender. (When educated men turned their attention to their own sex, they generally viewed men as too divided by differences of wealth, education, social standing, ability, and other factors to fall into a single category, a judgment that continues in much gender scholarship today, which generally uses the plural "masculinities" rather than the singular "masculinity.") Aristotle (384–322 BCE), for example, tended to view human anatomy and physiology on a single scale, describing women as imperfect or misbegotten males, born when something was less than perfect during conception and pregnancy, a conceptualization that has been labeled the "one-sex model" and that remained influential in Christian Europe and the Islamic world until the seventeenth century. Similar ideas developed in India, though with a more religious cast. In later Vedic literature, all fetuses began as male until malignant spirits turned some of them into females, an idea that led to male-producing ceremonies, held during the third month of pregnancy. Greek philosophy, the Vedas, and similar foundational texts from other cultures—including a handful written by women, such as the Confucian court historian and imperial adviser Ban Zhao (c. 50–c. 115 CE)—would thus be a good launching point, allowing you to emphasize the ways in which the ideas and opinions of a small share of the population came to be regarded as religious truth or scientific fact or "nature" and thus structured societies, a process that continues today. (*Sharing the World Stage* includes Ban Zhao and her brother Ban Gu as one of its paired biographies, but it has to skip the classical Greeks because no Greek woman left enough writings for even half a chapter.) The constructed nature of all norms and categories is a central insight of queer theory, a theme you could follow throughout the course.

If you prefer to have more than a minuscule number of female-authored texts for your students to read early in the course, you could begin in the postclassical (sometimes called the medieval or intermediate) period, say around 1000, when the Japanese court lady who became known as Murasaki Shikibu (973–1014?) wrote *The Tale of Genji*, the founding masterpiece of Japanese literature, and the lady-in-waiting Sei Shōnagon wrote a journal of commentary called *The Pillow Book* (covering the years 986–1000 CE); the German canoness Hrotsvitha of Gandersheim (c. 935– c. 1002) wrote plays, histories, and poetry in Latin; the Byzantine emperor's daughter Anna Comnena (1083–1148) wrote a narrative history of her father's period of rule; and various female Hindu *bhakti* poets wrote songs expressing their devotion to Krishna and other deities. The *Women in World History* website at the Center for History and New Media (CHNM) has selections from *The Tale of Genji*, *The Pillow Book*, and the bhakti poets, the earliest works by women that it includes. Comnena's history is available in English translation, as are most of the works of Hrotsvitha. Fictional stories, histories, and poetry by male authors with which to compare these abound. Artistic sources in many media—sculpture, bas reliefs, manuscript illuminations, paintings—survive in increasing numbers from this era, providing evidence of women's as well as men's actions. As with written sources, these are skewed toward the elite and idealized, but some depict more ordinary people going about their daily tasks. Written sources about actual work, household economies, popular religious activities, and real families also begin to emerge in some places, which can augment normative and prescriptive sources. Inclusion of multiple perspectives and diverse voices would then become a theme for the rest of the course as well.

You could follow the standard periodization in world history about important turning points and begin around 1500. Some women's historians, most prominently Judith Bennett, have emphasized continuities rather than dramatic change for women across the great divide of 1500, especially in Europe, but in global terms the movement of large numbers of people over vast distances disrupted existing patterns of marriage and family life and led to new patterns, just as the animals, plants, and germs they brought with them disrupted the ecosphere during the Columbian Exchange.[4] Although authorities often tried to keep groups apart, because the vast majority of merchants, conquerors, slaves, and settlers who traveled great distances were men, in many parts of the world a *mestizo* culture emerged in which not only ethnicity, but also religions, family patterns, cultural traditions, foodways, and languages blended. Women acted as intermediaries between local and foreign cultures, sometimes gaining great advantages for themselves and their children through their contact with dominant foreigners, though also sometimes suffering greatly as their contact with foreigners began when they were sold or given as gifts by their families, or taken forcibly.

For a course that begins around 1500 you could use the second volume of *Sharing the World Stage*, or you could assign a brief general world history textbook to provide a framework. I (Urmi) have used Robert Marks's *The Origins of the Modern World* alongside primary documents, which highlight the experiences of women that can get lost in broad world historical narratives.[5] I assign accounts of the conquest of the Americas by Spanish men, and I ask students to read between the lines to imagine the role of women as intermediaries and caretakers. Spanish conquerors, including Hernán Cortés and Bernal Díaz del Castillo, often mention their dependence on Native American women, such as Malintzin / Doña Marina, a Nahua woman who served as Cortés's translator and companion. Studying the role of women in narratives of colonial conquest reveals the complex politics of pre-Columbian empires in the Americas, in addition to highlighting issues of gender and sexuality in early cross-cultural encounters. The migration of large numbers of men also had an influence on gender structures in the areas they left. Two-thirds of the slaves carried across the Atlantic from Africa were male, with female slaves more likely to become part of the trans-Saharan trade or stay in West Africa, which reinforced polygyny. In northwestern Europe, male migration reinforced an existing pattern of late marriage and large numbers of women who remained single. The *Women in World History* website at CHNM provides original sources on many of these topics, including slavery, gender, and race in co-

lonial Latin America, and cultural contact in southern Africa. Works by
Judith Carney and John Thornton show the role of enslaved women in
transporting African foods and knowledge systems to the Americas, and
changes in gendered divisions of labor in food production in West Africa
during the Atlantic slave trade.[6] A course that starts with Columbus could
make gender and the environment a major theme, following this up to
modern ecofeminism. Or it could highlight slavery or cultural hybridity,
topics that have not lost any resonance.

The goods that were carried in the new international trading networks
also shaped gender, which in turn influenced that trade. Consumer goods
such as sugar and coffee required vast amounts of heavy labor, leading to
the development of plantation economies in tropical areas with largely
male slave workforces, along with the destruction of indigenous economies and native plant species. These slaves wore clothing made from cloth
that was often produced in European households, where traditional gender
divisions of labor were broken down because of the demands of the international marketplace. The new consumer goods—foodstuffs, clothing,
household furnishings—were purchased by middle- and upper-class Europeans and their descendants in North America and Australia, with wom-
en's roles in such households gradually becoming more oriented toward
consumption rather than production. Class status was signified by the
amount and quality of goods in one's home, all of which required purchase,
cleaning, care, and upkeep, which became the work—though unpaid—
of the women of a household, aided perhaps by a servant or two. Thus a
course that begins around 1500 could emphasize material culture.

You could start in the late eighteenth century, the era that may have
seen the beginning of modern sexuality, the modern family, and modern
gender relations, along with the rest of modernity. *A Global History of Sexuality: The Modern Era* does just this, beginning with the formation of
nation-states that resulted from the Atlantic revolutions, in which new
notions of national belonging and citizenship led to an increased focus on
sexual and gender identities along with enhanced regulation of sexuality by
institutions and societal norms.[7] The creation and celebration of national
varieties of masculinity—along with denigrations of the masculinity of

others—provide a strong explanatory value for much of modern history, including imperialism, the First World War, and the Cold War, and could be one theme to follow throughout the course. Rudyard Kipling's poetry might be too easy a source for this, but Walt Whitman's poem "Years of the Modern" (1865), an ode in praise (or seemingly in praise) of the "average man" and his "daring foot" that colonizes the world, could work well, especially if set against Gandhi's *Indian Self Rule* (1909) or other of his writings, many of which talk about women's as well as men's roles.

Many historians also trace modern understandings of race to the late eighteenth century, when educated Europeans combined earlier ideas about differences between human groups based on social standing, place of origin, religion, skin color, temperament, and other characteristics into the single schema "race," with four or five basic groups. Race was understood as inherited through the blood and was deeply gendered and sexualized. In the Caribbean, for example, men and women of each "race" were thought to have distinct sexual characteristics, inflected by class. Lower-class English women, in the opinion of the planter Edward Long, were "remarkably fond of the blacks" and would "contaminate English blood" with racial mixture. Such mixing, in the minds of many, led to foppish and beardless men and seductive, hypersexual women. Thus a course that began in the eighteenth century could make race a second key theme as it discusses imperialism, migration, and other transnational processes. The gendered division of labor is a natural third theme for a course that begins in the late eighteenth century, as you trace various patterns of industrialization, de-industrialization, and globalization to the present. Sources for this are everywhere.

As you can see, any number of starting points would allow you to create a good course. Whatever you decide, you need to make students aware of why you started when you did, as well as at least occasionally mention why you are organizing the course within certain periods. If you end the course before the present, you need to explain that too. Dividing the past into meaningful periods is something that historians do, and periodization is a historical thinking skill that students can learn. Historians of women, gender, and sexuality have been better at critiquing existing models of periodization than creating new ones, so you might as well bring your students into the discussion, for their untrained eyes might be better at seeing new chronological patterns than your more experienced ones. Chronologically organized courses often include specific themes, such as material culture, theory/practice, the environment, or race, either as ways to highlight what is important about certain periods or as guiding principles for the whole course. As with changing your depth of focus, integrating certain themes can make the course more meaningful for your students, providing examples of intersectionality and allowing them to connect it with what they are learning in other courses.

Instead of choosing themes to guide a chronologically organized course, you could flip this on its head and organize the course thematically, with change over time embedded within the themes. This would reinforce the central concept in feminist history that gender always intersects with other structures and institutions. My (Merry's) *Gender in History: Global Perspectives* provides one way to do this, with chapters on the family, economic life, ideas and norms, religion, political life, education and culture, and sexuality, again a seven-part organization that fits easily into a semester.[8] (The book also has a chronological table of contents if you want to use it that way.) Within each of your themes, you would then investigate ways in which what it meant to be male and female were shaped by such aspects of society as economic or religious structures, and how this changed over time. You would also explore the reverse—how gender in turn shaped work, for example, or religious institutions. You would not have to cover the whole sweep from the Paleolithic to now in every theme, but choose examples that make the most sense or are especially significant. The book does this, discussing the Paleolithic and Neolithic within the context of economic life and religion, but not in other chapters, and it spends more time on the modern era in the chapters on politics and sexuality. As with courses organized chronologically, you could begin with general points about the theme and then turn to examples from different eras and cultures, noting both distinctions among them and links between them, and suggesting possible reasons for variations among cultures and among different social, ethnic, and racial groups within one culture. Discussed in the book, for example, are various ways in which the rhetoric of motherhood has been used both to limit women's sphere of action and to expand it; in early twentieth-century Japan women were urged to be "good wives, wise mothers" by staying out of the workplace or public life, while in late twentieth-century Argentina the "Mothers of the Plaza de Mayo" used their status as mothers as a way to claim the right to publicly protest government abductions and killings. Writings from Japanese women who supported and opposed the domestic ideal and from Argentine women who supported and opposed the protests would allow you to zero in on individuals, as well as provide original sources for your students to analyze.

Both chronological and thematic organizations thus offer ways to structure your course that will make sense to students, especially if you bring them into the process along the way. Doing so will also reinforce the point that history means *constructing* a past, not just memorizing a bunch of facts for a test. If that is the only thing they remember from your course ten years later, you will have done a great job.

—— *Chapter Four* ——

Incorporating Key Issues

THEORY AND CONCEPTS FROM WOMEN'S,
GENDER, AND SEXUALITY STUDIES

AFTER CHOOSING A TITLE and determining how you in-
tend to organize the course, you will need to consider our fourth
design principle: *incorporating key issues from women's, gender,
and sexuality studies*. Historians who study women, gender, and
sexuality generally draw from a large body of theory from wom-
en's studies, feminist studies, gender studies, feminist literary
criticism, queer theory, and postcolonial and transnational feminist theory. These fields encompass a broad range of methodologies and disciplines, resulting in a range of theoretical positions
that draw from this multidisciplinary group of studies.

Deciding how much content you should include from disciplines outside of history, and how deeply you want to engage
with concepts and theories from women's, gender, and sexuality studies, depends on your own background and interest in
theory and your intentions in designing the course. A course
that focuses on issues of women could engage very little with
outside disciplines, while a course that emphasizes gender as an
analytical concept would require teaching about the develop-

ment of gender theory and its utility in studying the past. Of course, this decision also depends on the academic background of your students and the level of theory they would be able to handle without detracting from their study of historical developments, change and continuity over time, and global patterns and processes. But even if you do not assign readings in theory to your students, you will need to incorporate some key issues, all of which we discuss in this chapter: the social and cultural construction of gender; patriarchy and heteronormativity; public/private dichotomies; intersectionality, hybridity, and difference; voice and agency; sexual and gender identities; and discourse and representation. There are numerous ways to integrate these complex and challenging topics at strategic points in the course in ways that work for students who have little to no background in women's and gender studies, as well as for students who have powerful personal and political commitments to these issues.

You could design a course that foregrounds theory. Formative scholarship of the 1970s and 1980s, including works by Gayle Rubin, Michel Foucault, Nancy Chodorow, Chandra Talpade Mohanty, and others, can help introduce students to major themes and concepts that you will discuss throughout the course. Or you could start even earlier. Older works such as Mary Wollstonecraft's *A Vindication of the Rights of Woman* (1792), John Stuart Mill's *The Subjection of Women* (1869), Frederick Engels's "The Origin of the Family, Private Property, and the State" (1884), Sigmund Freud's *Three Essays on the Theory of Sexuality* (1909), and Simone de Beauvoir's *The Second Sex* (1952) are instructive in demonstrating the intellectual history of feminist theory, as it developed in Western Europe. Many scholars of feminist or women's studies include these historical works at the start of their course as foundational texts, and you could as well. However, in history courses that engage deeply with the historical context of the periods in which texts were written, it is more intellectually consistent to include these later on, at the appropriate chronological point. Of course, the same could be said about scholarship from the 1970s and 1980s, especially if your course covers these decades in detail.

There are a number of ways to include ideas and concepts from women's, gender, and sexuality studies without starting with a heavy dose of theoretical works. In a course that is organized chronologically, including a short conceptual piece to supplement the content of each period would help students to learn how to read the particular texts with certain theoretical positions in mind. Similarly, in a course that is organized thematically, scholarship from women's, gender, and sexuality studies could ground the themes that are covered. In introductory-level courses, you could present a short lecture that introduces theoretical concepts, then focus on them in discussions of historical articles and primary documents. Advanced students may be able to read complex theoretical arguments alongside historical articles and primary documents. We have found that students who take courses that are focused on issues of women and gender are often very interested in discussing current issues, and they are used to doing so if they have taken courses in women's studies or feminist studies departments. Discussing concepts and theoretical positions as they relate to present-day issues enables students to gain a solid understanding of these ideas, so they are better equipped to use them as analytical tools when studying the past.

If you do want to include some readings on theory, a good collection is Carole R. McCann and Seung-kyung Kim's *Feminist Theory Reader: Local and Global Perspectives*.[1] This comprehensive volume is commonly used in courses that introduce major themes, theories, and concepts in feminist studies. It includes numerous short essays that could supplement historical content, and it is especially useful in helping students to engage with global issues and debates. (Many of the articles mentioned in this chapter are included in this volume.)

In order for students to grasp the social and cultural construction of gender, you can begin with a discussion of how they currently understand basic terms such as "gender," "feminism," and "patriarchy," and then supplement their ideas with formal definitions from leading scholars in women's, gender, and feminist studies. Starting a course with an overview of key theoretical positions and concepts enables students to grapple with the complexity and diversity of meanings of terms they may take for granted. Beginning a course with a piece such as Joan Scott's "Gender: A Useful Category of Historical Analysis" provides students with a good overview of the complexity of gender theory, the historiography of women's and gender studies, and major questions and debates in these fields.[2] Jennifer Baumgardner and Amy Richards's essay "What Is Feminism?" and bell hooks's "Understanding Patriarchy" give clear overviews of these concepts, grounded in examples that are accessible to undergraduates who do not have a background in reading heavy theoretical texts.[3]

Alongside these works, introducing students to works in masculinity studies provides a way of balancing their views of patriarchy and heteronormativity. Jack Halberstam's introduction to *Female Masculinity*, R. W. Connell's "Change among the Gatekeepers: Men, Masculinities, and Gender Equality in the Global Arena," or excerpts from Todd Reeser's instructive volume *Masculinities in Theory: An Introduction* present accessible explanations of the ways in which masculinity has been defined and understood in various contexts.[4] This scholarship demonstrates the diversity and variety of ways in which masculinity is understood and performed across cultures. As Reeser argues, "Cross-cultural or cross-temporal differences make us aware of masculinity as particularly relative, since we come to see that what is taken for granted is not at all a given, but a fabrication or construct of a given historical and cultural context."[5] Readings on masculinity are useful in courses that focus on the early-modern or modern periods, as well as those that extend across the longue durée of human history.

In courses that include a broader chronology that begins in the Paleolithic, you may want to incorporate anthropological perspectives. Beginning with Joan Scott's essay immediately raises questions about the origins of patriarchy, a topic that students are often eager to discuss. Scott's outline of how theorists of patriarchy have explained its origins shows how a historical perspective challenges these explanations. Reading various interpretations of how and when patriarchal social systems emerged in different contexts urges students to think about processes of historical change, while considering possible causes or explanations for what would eventually emerge as a dominant global pattern. When did patriarchy begin? Are there patterns that we can discern as marking the rise of patriarchal societies independently, throughout the globe? Many world historians, and world history textbooks, draw connections between the rise of agricultural societies and the rise of patriarchal social systems. Some feminist theorists and women's historians also link patriarchy with agriculture, or with the development of public/private dichotomies in early cities and states, in which men were associated with the public sphere and women with the private. Alternatively, the anthropologist and primatologist Richard Wrangham argues that gendered divisions of labor emerged much earlier, with the evolution of *Homo erectus* about eight million years ago, when humans began eating cooked food. In *Catching Fire: How Cooking Made Us Human*, he links the use of fire and the necessity of maintaining a hearth as central to the growth of gendered divisions of labor in the majority of human societies.[6] Other portrayals of hunter-gatherer societies from across the globe also depict a division of labor based on sex, though some of these present this as an essentialized man-the-hunter / woman-the-gatherer picture while others focus on the development of varied cultural practices. Arguments about the origins of patriarchy are fraught with conjecture and rarely result in a consensus, but introducing students to them allows them to grapple with the disconnect between the sometimes overly uniform big history narratives or grand theories, and the more specialized studies of cultural historians, cultural anthropologists, and scholars of gender. Taking a long-term, world historical perspective does not necessarily mean presenting one single origin story for patriarchy, but instead multiple points in which material changes in human behaviors resulted in changes in social and cultural relationships.

In addition to debating when and why patriarchy emerged as the dominant system of social and political relations in most human societies, you should also discuss how gender and sexual systems changed over time and interrelated with other structures of inequality and difference. By doing so, gender and sexuality will be integrated into your discussion of familiar world historical developments, including the spread of world religions, the growth of global trade routes, and the rise of empires. But you should also present examples of societies that somehow diverged from standard patterns. Students often have a progressive notion that the gross inequalities of the past are changing in the present. After all, in their lifetimes and the lifetimes of their mothers, they have witnessed a general trend in the growth of rights for women and the rapid rise of support for gay and lesbian civil rights. As a result, many students in North America and Europe conclude that any sort of a public role for women or any acceptance of same-sex relationships or transgender individuals is a modern phenomenon. If they have thought about the reasons for these changes, they see them as the result of activism and education, and perhaps vaguely as the result of the spread of Western liberal ideas. Providing them with examples of the diverse ways in which human societies have viewed and organized sex and gender, and how these have changed over time as a result of various global and ecological processes, highlights questions about the structures that enable all types of inequalities, rather than implying a triumphant narrative of Western liberal values. In addition, over the course of the term, students will often change their views on the inherency or inevitability of patriarchal systems. Students are often very interested in societies that have alternatives to patriarchal and heteronormative structures, such as those with matrilineal kinship systems or more than two genders. Sabrina Ramet's edited collection *Gender Reversals and Gender Cultures* or Gilbert Herdt's *Third Sex, Third Gender* include historical and contemporary examples that fascinate students, with chapters written by historians and anthropologists.[7]

Some concepts that have been central in gender and sexuality scholarship are particularly important to include in courses that focus on the modern period. One of these is the relationship between ideas of race and gender and scientific developments. Studying the European Enlightenment and Scientific Revolution through the lens of gender offers students a critical view of the evolution of modern institutions. An iconic figure such as Sara Baartman, a Khoikhoi woman who was exhibited across England, Ireland, and France because of her large buttocks, provides students with a concrete example that illustrates the context of other scientific concepts developed by the French natural scientist Georges Cuvier. Presenting the history of eighteenth-century developments in the natural sciences alongside a biographical account of Baartman, such as Clifton Crais and Pamela Scully's *Sara Baartman and the Hottentot Venus: A Ghost Story and a Biography*, is an effective way of showing how interconnected ideas about race and gender shaped modern scientific theories.[8] Articles that document the relationship between the development of scientific ideas and theories of gender difference based on biological differences serve to complicate narratives of scientific progress that students may have learned prior to their university studies or in other classes. For example, Londa Schiebinger's "Why Mammals Are Called Mammals" and "Skeletons in the Closet" provide insight into the ways in which contemporary notions of gender shaped modern scientific theories.[9]

Issues of intersectionality, hybridity, and difference can be taught using a variety of readings from a range of literatures and disciplines. An effective way of introducing students to the concept of intersectionality is through reading concrete historical examples that illustrate how intersections of race, class, gender, sexuality, and nationality complicate women's situations in diverse contexts. Further, the role of historical social and political processes, such as those in slave societies and colonial spaces, provides a greater depth to understanding the scope of intersectionality and range of factors that contribute to the diverse experiences of women. For example, Evelyn Brooks Higginbotham's "African American Women's History and the Metalanguage of Race" focuses on the experience of African American women in the United States, while Mrinalini Sinha's "Gender and Nation" discusses the relationship between competing feminisms and nationalisms.[10]

Teaching about difference and hybridity can be effectively addressed in studying feminist movements in different regional and historical contexts. When studying women and feminism in the modern Middle East, students could begin with the introduction to Lila Abu-Lughod's edited volume *Remaking Women: Feminism and Modernity in the Middle East*, alongside a chapter from the volume.[11] Articles in this volume highlight the complex identities that emerged across the Middle East. Students are often eager to discuss debates about veiling, which can be blended with detailed critiques, such as Leila Ahmed's "The Discourse of the Veil." Pairing this essay with a primary document, such as Marjane Satrapi's graphic memoir *Persepolis*, portrays the complex intersection of identities based on gender, religion, and nation.[12] In a course that engages more deeply with transnational feminism and discourses of postcolonialism, Chandra Talpade Mohanty's key essay, "Under Western Eyes: Feminist Scholarship and Colonial Discourses," together with her reassessment of her work in *Feminism without Borders: Decolonizing Theory, Practicing Solidarity*, shows how a person's identity, positionality, and ideas can change over time.[13] Readings from other disciplines can deepen your presentation of issues surrounding difference. The multidisciplinarity of feminist studies provides ample works from fields such as anthropology, sociology, and religious studies. Abu-Lughod's ethnography of the Awlad 'Ali Bedouins provides a tangible example of the ways that gendered behaviors and power relationships are transformed by historical change, especially by the rise of modern states and capitalist economies.[14]

Issues of voice and agency can be taught in several ways. Advanced students might be interested in reading Gayatri Chakravorty Spivak's classic "Can the Subaltern Speak?"[15] For a more general course, concepts of voice and agency can be illustrated in various historical contexts. A good explanation of the issues of locating voices of women is in the introduction to *Contesting Archives: Finding Women in the Sources*.[16] Assigning the introduction, along with a chapter from the volume, would provide students with a historically grounded example of how scholars can assess the agency of marginalized women. The volume includes short essays that illustrate the methods scholars have used to find women's voices in a range of contexts, including early modern Spain, Mexico during the colonial period and nineteenth century, nineteenth-century Tunis, communist Poland, Progressive-Era California, and beyond.

Determining the agency of enslaved women raises additional questions. My students have been very engaged when I (Urmi) have asked them to assess the strengths and limitations of Trevor Burnard's analysis of enslaved men and women as presented in Thomas Thistlewood's journals of eighteenth-century Jamaica. Burnard is explicit in outlining his approach, and my students have engaged in debates about his interpretation of the motivations of various enslaved women, and his analysis of the psychological implications of the traumatic experiences that they endured.[17]

Theory developed in women's, gender, and feminist studies is especially crucial in teaching about sexual and gender identities. The literature on lesbian feminism that developed in the 1970s and 1980s, led by theorists such as Charlotte Bunch, Gayle Rubin, Adrienne Rich, Monique Wittig, and Kate Millet, provides a framework that encourages students to question their assumptions about lesbianism and to consider it as distinct from the heteronormative feminism or the gay and lesbian rights movements that they have grown up witnessing. Charlotte Bunch's "Lesbians in Revolt" and Cheshire Calhoun's "Separating Lesbian Theory from Feminist Theory" offer students ways of thinking of lesbianism beyond defining it as sexual behavior. Bunch considers lesbianism as a "political choice" that is "central to destroying our sexist, racist, capitalist, imperial system."[18] Queer theory is also important, including Gayle Rubin's "Thinking Sex: Notes for a Radical Theory of the Politics of Sexuality," Eve Sedgwick's *Epistemology of the Closet*, and works by Judith Butler.[19] Alongside these, excerpts from historical accounts of gay or lesbian identities, such as George Chauncey's *Gay New York*, John D'Emilio and Estelle Friedman's *Intimate Matters: A History of Sexuality in America*, Cindy Patton and Benigno Sánchez-Eppler's *Queer Diasporas*, or Sokari Ekine and Hakima Abbas's *Queer African Reader* would give students the tools to have meaningful discussions about the role of sexuality, historically and cross-culturally.[20] Considering theories of gender and sexuality with studies that focus on the specific historical construction of identities provides rich material for students to consider multiple and conflicting ideas about the fluidity of sexuality. Comparing Bunch's arguments to those made by D'Emilio in "Capitalism and Gay Identity" would allow them to see diverse ways of understanding the rise of gay and lesbian identities in the twentieth century.[21] These interpretations raise difficult questions about the relationship between capitalism and gay identity, as well as differences in the construction of gay male identities compared to lesbian identities.

In a course that is organized thematically, you could choose themes that are grounded in theoretical concepts. An advanced course that focuses on the post-1750 period could include themes such as "Constructing Gender," "Gendering the Body," "Representing the Body," and "Performing Gender." Readings on these themes would include theory as well as historical monographs or essays. A section on performing gender could include Judith Butler's essay "Performative Acts and Gender Constitution: An Essay in Phenomenology and Feminist Theory," combined with historical examples from various regions, including selections from Antoinette Burton's *Dwelling in the Archive: Women Writing House, Home, and History in Late Colonial India*, Chauncey's *Gay New York*, and Ekine and Abbas's *Queer African Reader*.[22]

Courses that focus on the modern period can also engage closely with debates and theories surrounding transformations in gender and sexuality in relation to the rise of global capitalism. While scholarship in gender and feminist studies may refer to Marxist concepts, it often lacks a historical treatment of Marx and the spread of his ideas. A course on women and gender in world history is a unique setting for discussing Marx as a historical figure, the spread of Marxism as a global process, and the convergence of Marxism and feminism. This could be done effectively by reading Marx alongside primary documents by Marxist feminists such as Alexandra Kollontai, combined with scholarship in feminist studies, for example, Heidi Hartmann's "The Unhappy Marriage of Marxism and Feminism: Towards a More Progressive Union."[23]

Whatever the chronological spread or organization of your course, using images is a powerful way of helping students to understand the role of symbols in the cultural construction of gender and sexuality, and why issues of representation and discourse have been so important in feminist theory. Studying historical examples of these representations enable students to connect the past and present, and to critically consider their position regarding contemporary debates about the significance of symbols and representations that have become increasingly politicized on college campuses. More broadly, images and illustrations provide excellent material to begin discussions that are also based on reading documents and analytical essays.

Representations of women, gender, and sexuality are usually complicated in their depictions of race, ethnicity, and social status. Racialized portrayals of women emerged among colonial artists in the British Empire, for example in images of *sati* (widow burning), publicized in travel accounts in the seventeenth through nineteenth centuries. In Spanish and Portuguese colonies in the Americas, notions of racial purity, social class, and honor are portrayed in eighteenth-century *casta* paintings, in which artists rendered their views of the variety of categories of children of mixed ancestry. European images of Islamic households, harems, and slave auctions also present an excellent source of discussion of Orientalist representations of Islamic culture. These images could be paired with critical readings such as Edward Said's *Orientalism* or selections from Nell Irvin Painter's *The History of White People*.[24] Similarly, critiques of the supposed objectivity of photographic images can be seen in the medical photography of Louis Agassiz. Literary criticism, such as Sander Gilman's essay "Black Bodies, White Bodies," can help students in critically evaluating these sources.[25]

The Cold War era presents numerous opportunities for engaging with visual sources. Communist posters during the Great Leap Forward and Cultural Revolution, alongside a study of the Marriage Law of 1950, show how Maoist supporters understood the status of women under Communism. Images of Soviet and American women during the Cold War highlight the ways in which consumerism was central to cultural contests. In *Fashioneast: The Spectre That Haunted Socialism*, Djurdja Bartlett presents a compelling analysis combined with a wealth of imagery.[26]

Films are also instructive in showing the power of representation in the twentieth century. Clips from *Birth of a Nation* (1915) clearly show links between fears of interracial sexual relations and the rise of white supremacy in the United States. Representations of two-spirit identity in *Little Big Man* (1970) illustrate the ways in which Americans linked sexual and gender identities during an era of sexual revolution. Contemporary representations of prostitution in South Asia, such as in Thomas Kelly's *Fallen Angels* or the film *Born into Brothels* (2004), raise questions about representations of poverty and sexuality among artists who are portraying these peoples to Western audiences.[27]

There are many ways to blend history with theories and concepts from the vast, multidisciplinary literature in women's, gender, feminist, and sexuality studies. In your classroom, you will probably find a self-selected group of students who are drawn to courses on women, gender, and sexuality for personal or political reasons, and often a substantial number of students will have a background in women's or feminist studies. Use their expertise! They can be quite helpful in taking the lead in discussions of theoretical questions and can bring in information from their studies of women or gender in other disciplines, while history majors in the class are often able to identify ways of connecting these ideas to historical realities.

PART II

Modifying Existing Courses

IN PART II, we discuss issues involved with modifying existing courses because of changes in the field, changes in your interests as an instructor, or changes in modes of instruction. We set out three design principles: *integrating gender more fully as a category of analysis, globalizing a regionally based course so that it has a broader geographic base*, and *incorporating feminist pedagogy as you move online.*

———— *Chapter Five* ————

Integrating Gender More Fully as a Category of Analysis

BEYOND "ADD MEN AND STIR"

THE EXPERIENCES OF WOMEN, and of nonwhite men, were often first included in college and high school history textbooks within boxed features, or at the very most in separate sections distinct from the main narrative, an approach that in terms of women was sarcastically labeled "add women and stir." The development of gender history out of women's history means that instructors who have been in the field for a while might face the opposite problem: They have a course in women's history that has worked quite well, but have decided to transform it into a course in gender history. How can they (or you, if this is your situation) do so in a way to avoid just tacking on a few units about men and masculinity, but also not have to start from scratch? This chapter provides guidance on our fifth design principle, *integrating gender more fully as a category of analysis*. Most of this chapter's examples are topics that are staples in general world history courses, such as the rise and spread of text-based religions and the process of imperialism, so you can use them if you wish to add or better integrate gender and sexuality into your world history survey as well.

The first step might be to go halfway, to a course on "women and gender," which is actually a common title for many existing courses, as well as textbooks and other materials designed for these courses. In fact, no matter what its title, your existing course in women's history may already be a course on women and gender, as most women's history courses also examine gender as a system of socially constructed power relations, gender ideologies affecting both women and men, and the intersection of gender hierarchies and identities with those of ethnicity, status, religion, and so on. Keep these units. Of the units that focus more specifically on women, decide which are the strongest, and keep them as well. There is nothing wrong with sometimes focusing just on women, or just on men. Of those units you think are weaker, or in need of updating, decide if the topic is something that your students should learn about in a world history course. If it is, design a new approach that uses gender as a tool of analysis as well as a subject, and pick new readings and other materials. What follows are a few examples that can serve as models.

In a women's history course that has a broad chronological scope and often in world history surveys you probably already discuss classical Athens, because it has traditionally been regarded as the intellectual and political foundation of Western culture, left so many sources, and, for women's history, provides such a juicy example of a "golden age" that was not very positive for women. So you just need to shift your focus slightly. Lin Foxhall's concise *Studying Gender in Classical Antiquity* is an excellent overview of the ways gender was linked to other sociopolitical structures, beginning with the household; it also discusses how to interpret the wide range of sources that scholars use to investigate the ancient Mediterranean world.[1] As Foxhall notes, in Athens, as in all ancient societies, most free people married, and the size of the household depended on social status, with wealthier households containing more relatives, servants, and slaves than poorer ones. (This might seem self-evident to you, but it will not be to most of your students, who are used to a situation in which poorer families and households are often larger than wealthy ones.) Whatever a household's size or composition, everyone living within it, including adult children and servants, was under the authority of the male head of household, a common situation in the ancient world, so in this Athens can serve as a typical example.

What made Athens unusual is the one thing your students may know about it, that it was a democracy in which, beginning in the sixth century BCE, adult male citizens had a real say in political and military decisions. Enslaved men and the immigrants known as *metics*—groups that made up the majority of the male population in the city—had no voice. Neither did any women (at least formally), and because citizenship was handed down within families from father to son, it was very important to Athenian citizen men that their sons be their own. Citizen wives and daughters were increasingly secluded in special parts of the house and appeared in public only for religious festivals, funerals, and perhaps the theater (there is a debate about this among historians), though enslaved and metic women walked the streets and marketplaces as they worked and socialized. Thus instead of being simply an example of misogyny—though there is plenty of that in Athenian sources—Athens can become an example of the way citizenship is inflected by gender and by family relationships, a theme you can continue to trace throughout the course right up to the present. As Dagmar Herzog comments about contemporary Europe, "The entire complex of issues surrounding European identities and citizenships, with all the accompanying assumptions about appropriate inclusions and exclusions, now rests with remarkable frequency on sex-related concerns."[2] Similarly, this focus on differences *among* men and *among* women as well as between them will be a theme you can come back to again and again, whether you are teaching a gender history course or a world history survey.

Classical Athens also provides an excellent example of understandings of sexuality and sexual identity that are very different from the ones with which your students are familiar. Part of an adolescent citizen's training in adulthood was supposed to entail a hierarchical tutorial and sexual relationship with an older man, who most likely was married and may have had other female sexual partners as well. Sexuality was thus primarily a matter of actions, not identities. Such relationships were often celebrated in literature and art, in part because the Athenians regarded perfection as possible only in the male. The perfect body was that of the young male, and perfect love was between a younger and an older man, not between a man and an imperfect woman. This love was supposed to become intellectualized and nonsexual once the adolescent became an adult, the type of attachment we still term "platonic," based on Plato's (427–347 BCE) suspicion of the power of sexual passion. How often actual sexual relations between men or between men and women approached the ideal in Athens is very difficult to say, as most of our sources are prescriptive, idealized, or fictional, but this makes them perfect for the study of changing sexual norms. Thomas Hubbard's *Homosexuality in Greece and Rome: A Sourcebook* provides a wealth of these, including well-known writings by Plato and Sappho along with less well-known texts such as graffiti, comic fragments, magical papyri, medical treatises, and selected artistic evidence, plus valuable introductions.[3]

Another important premodern topic you most likely already discuss is the rise of text-based religions such as Buddhism, Christianity, and Islam, and the ways religious teachings have been used both to strengthen and to question existing social and gender structures, because they provide ideas about divinely sanctioned hierarchy as well as complementarity and equality. For example, the Buddha (566–486 BCE) taught that the best way of life is one of moderation and meditation, a rejection of worldly concerns and a search for enlightenment. In theory, the Buddhist path to enlightenment (*nirvana* or *nibbana*) is open to all, regardless of sex or caste or class; one needs simply to rid oneself of all desires, which may be accomplished progressively through a series of deaths and rebirths. Gender and class differences are part of the world that keeps one from enlightenment and not part of the true nature of existence, a teaching that has attracted contemporary people around the world to Buddhism, or to Buddhist-inflected practices such as yoga and meditation. Such egalitarianism conflicted with other teachings, however, for women were also viewed as a dangerous threat to men's achieving enlightenment and in some writings were regarded as not capable of achieving enlightenment unless they first became men.

The conflict between these two notions emerged during the Buddha's lifetime. The Buddha taught that renouncing the world in favor of the life of a monk or nun made one spiritually superior, and women wanted him to form an order of nuns to offer women the same opportunities for withdrawal from the world that his order of monks (the *sangha*) had for men. According to Buddhist tradition, the Buddha hesitated a long time, and finally established an order for nuns, but gave them special rules that stressed their subordinate status to monks and placed them clearly under male control. Despite these restrictions, women eagerly joined this new type of religious life, although communities of nuns never received the support that communities of monks did. In some places where Buddhism spread, women were (and are) prohibited from being formally ordained, though whether this matters much to the women who renounce the world to follow Buddhist monastic practices and seek nirvana is unclear.[4]

Your course on women may already discuss Buddhist nuns, perhaps comparing them to Christian ones as monasticism in both religious traditions provided opportunities for women's leadership and escape from family life largely unavailable in the secular world. Renouncing the world meant (at least in theory) renouncing bodily desire for *both* men and women, however, which can provide you with an opportunity to focus on the body itself as a historical agent as you shift the focus to gender. As Liz Wilson has explored in *Charming Cadavers: Horrific Figurations of the Feminine in Indian Buddhist Hagiographic Literature*, many early Buddhist texts encourage men who wanted to be monks and achieve enlightenment to meditate on images of women's diseased, dying, or dead bodies in order to cultivate detachment from desire.[5] The male bodies celebrated in these texts are those that have achieved this difficult goal, becoming asexual and somewhat androgynous, qualities that are also often part of today's ideas about the Buddha himself. Jonathan Powers's *A Bull of a Man: Images of Masculinity, Sex, and the Body in Indian Buddhism*, by contrast, examines other early texts that present the Buddha and his monastic followers as powerful, virile, and sensual, paragons of masculinity with perfect bodies and heroic self-control.[6] Both of these books include translations of the works they study that will allow your students to examine embodied ideals of masculinity. The fact that these ideals are not consistent or uniform is a plus, as too often world religions are taught in ways that are ahistorical and reductive—Buddhists have the Four Noble Truths, Muslims the Five Duties of the Believer—rather than as the highly diverse and historically changing traditions that they are. Examining ideas about monastic manliness in the early centuries of Buddhism could also provide useful background for students seeking to understand the important—and sometimes violent—role that Buddhist monks play today in many parts of Asia, especially Thailand and Myanmar (Burma).

Moving into the modern period, it is hard to imagine a course that does not discuss colonialism and imperialism. So instead of your existing unit in a women's history course on women and imperialism or your unit in the world history survey that discusses imperialism primarily as a political and military venture, create one that focuses on how the process of empire building shaped gender and sexuality, as well as the reverse. This would include men and women as agents in imperial projects, and—to reflect new trends in research—would emphasize links between colonized areas and the metropole, thus moving beyond a binary of colonizer and colonized. Kathleen Wilson's *The Island Race: Englishness, Empire and Gender in the Eighteenth Century*, for example, examines ways in which English men's and women's perceptions of their English identity were shaped by colonial expansion and by notions of gender, and it would be a good reading with which to begin a unit on imperialism.[7] The whole book is probably too long, but it is really a series of case studies drawn both from Britain and across the Atlantic and Pacific worlds, so the introduction and one chapter would be enough. Wilson also explicitly notes that her book is not comprehensive, but instead discusses only *some* of the places where Britons' beliefs about their national character and destiny were produced, and suggests that readers might well want to examine others. Thus it makes an important methodological point true for all world history. Another possibility for a book that links colony and metropole is Zine Magubane's relatively short *Bringing the Empire Home: Race, Class, and Gender in Britain and Colonial South Africa*, which traces colonial images of blackness from South Africa to Britain and back again, noting the ways these influenced self-definitions of marginalized groups such as women, the poor, and Irish workers in Britain, and of blacks themselves in South Africa.[8] To include an example from beyond the British Empire, Julia Clancy-Smith and Frances Gouda's *Race, Gender, and Family Life in French and Dutch Colonialism* has essays on gendered colonial rhetoric and actual encounters in North and West Africa and Southeast Asia that work well with students.[9]

Imperialism was not simply a matter of discourse and representation, but of real bodies that interacted in all sorts of ways, including intermarriage, rape, prostitution, and other types of sexual relationships among individuals belonging to what were defined as different groups. That definition—along ethnic, religious, racial, or other lines—was itself gendered and sexualized. For example, the first appearance of the word "white" to describe a group of people in what became the United States was a 1691 Virginia law regarding prohibited sexual relations, which distinguished between "white" men and women and those who were "negroe, mulatto, or Indian." (Earlier Virginia laws about prohibited sex distinguished between "christian" and "negroe.") Similar "miscegenation" laws were passed in all of the southern colonies and some northern ones between 1700 and 1750, and later in Midwestern and Western states prohibiting marriages between whites and Native Americans, Chinese, Japanese, Filipinos, and Hawaiians as well as blacks. Though such laws were usually gender-neutral, what lawmakers were most worried about was, as the preamble to the Virginia law states, "negroes, mulattoes, and Indians intermarrying with English, or other white women" and the resultant "abominable mixture and spurious issue." On this, Peggy Pascoe's *What Comes Naturally: Miscegenation Law and the Making of Race in America* is both thorough and accessible to students, allowing them to see the way the United States fit with global patterns as it created racial hierarchies yet also developed its own distinctive dichotomous racial system, in which one drop of "black blood" made one not white.[10]

You could contrast this dichotomous racial system with that in the Spanish and Portuguese colonies, in which authorities created an ever more complex system of categories, called *castas*, for persons of mixed ancestry, based in theory on place of birth, assumed geographic origin, and status of one's father and mother, though in practice the categories were determined to a large extent by how one looked. The best-known representations of these castas are eighteenth-century paintings that show scenes of parents of different castas and the children such parents produced, which are always fascinating for students. Magal M. Carrera's *Imagining Identity in New Spain: Race, Lineage, and the Colonial Body in Portraiture and Casta Paintings* has a good selection of these, and they are widely available on the web.[11] Setting casta paintings alongside laws of the British North American colonies provides a good way to begin your discussion of the ways racial hierarchies, notions of gender, and fears about sex intersected in complex ways throughout the colonial world, and continue to shape the postcolonial one.[12] Or you could contrast the envisioned mixed-race families in casta paintings with those that actually developed in Spanish colonies by having students read a chapter from Jane Mangan's *Transatlantic Obligations: Creating the Bonds of Family in Conquest-Era Peru and Spain* or from Tony Ballantyne and Antoinette Burton's *Bodies in Contact: Rethinking Colonial Encounters in World History.*[13]

Along with modifying existing topics as you transform your course from women to gender or incorporate gender and sexuality into your world history survey, you can also add completely new topics or themes. The most obvious is masculinity, about which there are now hundreds of books and thousands of articles discussing nearly every society and era. Ulrike Strasser and Heidi Tinsman's article "It's a Man's World?," discussed in chapter 2, would be an excellent way to introduce your students to this issue and the literature.

Because of the long tradition of viewing men as differentiated, and because diversity of experience is such a strong emphasis in current gender scholarship, studies of masculinity often use the plural "masculinities" rather than the singular. They emphasize that all men construct their masculinity in relation not only to women, but also to other men, and that groups of men also vary widely in their ability to shape their own masculinity depending on their position in racial, class, and other power structures. Young male nationalists in postcolonial Africa, for example, were often successful at changing traditions through which older men had held power over them, such as unfavorable inheritance practices, adapting ideas they had learned through print and media, and often by their own experiences abroad. The new scholarship on masculinity is thus innovative in its recognition that men have and do gender, but it is traditional in its emphasis that the differences among men are so large and significant that generalizations are impossible. Although it is the exact counterpart to masculinity, "femininity" has not caught on as a term of scholarly study, perhaps because it is still seen as less open to variation than masculinity. A pluralized "femininities" has not generally emerged as the way to solve the problem, though there is no reason you cannot use "masculinities and femininities" in your course, or at least talk with your students about why the two words are not equally popular.

As you discuss the social construction of masculinities and femininities, it would be good to include a discussion of individuals who transcended the gender dichotomy by moving from one gender to another, rising above it, blending genders, creating their own gender, refusing to be categorized, or stumping those doing the categorization. These are individuals who now identify as transsexual, transgender, intersex, third gender, agender, or some other term, and in many places they have formed movements for equal rights. The trans movement is often associated with gay, lesbian, and bisexual groups (reflected in the LGBTQ acronym), though some trans people dispute this link, noting that the issue for them is gender, not sexual orientation. Given the recent flurry of attention to a few celebrities, your students might think that being trans was something new, but over the last twenty years, historians and anthropologists have discovered people in many of the world's cultures who were categorized as or understood themselves to be neither male nor female. Sometimes the designation was a temporary state, and sometimes a permanent condition. Some of these individuals were (and are) physically intersexed, and occasionally they were (and are) eunuchs, but more commonly they were (and are) morphologically male or female but understood to be something else.

Third and trans genders might have started, in fact, during the Paleolithic. Many cave paintings show groups of prey or predator animals with a masked human figure, usually judged to be a shaman, performing some sort of ritual. Sometimes the shaman is shown with what looks like a penis, and such figures used to be invariably described as men. More recently anthropologists have suggested that these figures may have been *gendered* male, but could have been a woman wearing a costume that included an artificial penis, as gender inversions are often part of many types of rituals and performances. Or the figure—and the actual shaman whom it may have represented—was understood as a third gender, neither male nor female, or both at the same time, transcending a gender boundary as well as the boundary between animals and humans or between the seen and unseen worlds.

Shamans understood to be neither male nor female can be found in many parts of the world in the more recent past than the Paleolithic, as can other third or transgender individuals. These include the *bissu* of South Sulawesi in Indonesia, linked to the androgynous creator deity, who carried out rituals to enhance and preserve the power and fertility of the rulers; the *hijra* of northern India, understood to have the power to grant fertility through their replication of the androgyny of the goddess Bahuchara Mata and of Lord Shiva, who perform blessings at marriages and the births of male children; the *quimbanda* of West Africa, who took the spirits of deceased ancestors into their heads and served as advisors to villagers and chiefs; *mahus* in Polynesia, who were morphologically male but performed rituals and work usually associated with women; and *babaylans* in the Philippines, who communicated with the spirit world and performed healing and foretelling rituals. The best known of these are found among Native American peoples, and the Europeans who first encountered them regarded them as homosexuals and called them *berdaches*, from an Arabic word for male prostitute. Now most scholars and activists choose to use the term "two-spirit people" and note that, though Europeans focused on their sexuality, two-spirit people are often distinguished from others by their work or religious roles, as well as their sexual activities. Two-spirit people were regarded as having both a male and female spirit, rather than the one spirit that most people had, and could thus mediate between the male and female world as well as the divine and human world. The difference was thus one of gender rather than sexuality.[14]

Studies of third and trans people in the past are not simply broadening historical scholarship, but are also proving politically useful, as people within the gay rights and trans movements in many parts of the world today use them to demonstrate the variety in indigenous understandings of gender and sexuality and to stress that demands for rights for homosexuals or trans people are not simply a Western import. Mahu, for example, was the name chosen for the Asian and Pacific Islander lesbian, gay, bisexual, and transgender student organization at UCLA. The 2014 feature-length documentary *Kuma Hina*, which focuses on a trans Native Hawaiian teacher and cultural leader, would be an excellent introduction for your students to this issue, as would *A Place in the Middle*, a shorter documentary on one of Kuma Hina's students.[15] Two-spirit groups are leading the movement to repeal Native American laws that prohibit same-sex marriage, such as the 2005 Diné Marriage Act of the Navaho Nation, which defines marriage as being only between a man and a woman. A web search will take you easily to online articles about the movement, though the comments sections invariably contain the same level of vitriol that you can find on any discussion of a sexual issue.

Adding new material will, of course, mean that you will have to let other things go, but that always happens when you update or revise a course for any reason, which is why we suggest starting by replacing units you are not very happy with now. (And keep in mind you can *never* be exhaustive in a world history course.) After you have made what might be fewer changes than you anticipated, your women's history course will focus primarily on gender, or your world history survey will incorporate gender and sexuality. Your students should be able to apply what they have learned in the new units to the entire course and to their other courses as well.

Chapter Six

Globalizing a Regionally Based Course

TEACHING WHAT YOU DO NOT KNOW

TOPICS OF WOMEN, gender, and sexuality transcend regional and national boundaries. This chapter provides guidance on our sixth design principle, *globalizing a regionally based course so that it has a broader geographic base*, in order to present a more inclusive history of gender identity and the diverse experiences of women. Whether you are attempting to globalize a course that now focuses on women, gender, and/or sexuality in the United States, China, Europe, or elsewhere, incorporating content that you are unfamiliar with presents difficulties. These are similar to the challenges that you might face when transitioning from a Western civilization course to world history, or from a course on modern East Asia to the modern world.

It is daunting for scholars who have focused exclusively on one region (which is most of us) to integrate a depth of knowledge of other areas into a course. How do you teach about a culture that you have never studied? How do you teach what you do not know? Knowing that whatever topics or materials you choose will become representative of a culture, how can you avoid essentializing cultures in diverse world regions? How do you balance difference and familiarity when studying the region where you are located? How can historians of Europe and the United States balance difference and familiarity, to avoid Orientalizing and yet not erase otherness? How can historians who focus on the subaltern balance uniqueness, intersectionality, and commonalities?

Approaching the topic of women, gender, and sexuality from a background in European or U.S. history presents different problems than coming from a regional specialization elsewhere in the world. Scholars who teach about "other" cultures (i.e., teach about areas outside of the United States in a classroom in the United States, or teach U.S. history outside of the United States) must confront the issue of breaking down preconceptions students might have about cultures and histories with which they are unfamiliar. By contrast, those who teach about a culture and history with which students have intimate experiences face the difficulty of getting students to question their knowledge and assumptions, especially about matters on which they have already formed a deep and personal understanding. Regardless of where you fall on this spectrum, a fundamental challenge is to provoke students to acknowledge their own positionality relative to the historical and cultural contexts that they are studying. At the start of a course, it is useful to have students describe their own position in history and to consider how their views developed in a particular context by acknowledging their national, ethnic, religious, socioeconomic, and educational backgrounds. This can be helpful in any world history course, but it is particularly so in a course on women, gender, and/or sexuality, as cultural attitudes about women and gender are especially dominant in shaping moral arguments about a society's treatment of women and normative gender roles. Your course may present a new set of complications and challenges to students because of their political beliefs and personal experiences. (For more on this, see chapter 8.)

Research on the history of women, gender, and sexuality has grown substantially in the past few decades, though most of this focuses on the United States and Europe. Measured by the books submitted for the American Historical Association's Joan Kelly Prize and the Berkshire Conference of Women Historians, the majority of scholarship produced in the United States concerns U.S. history, followed by British history, continental Europe in third place, and the rest of the world a very distant fourth. Studies of women and gender have become more prominent within regional specializations, however, such as studies of the modern Middle East, Latin America, and Africa.[1] Scholarship on women and gender in East Asia, especially China, has grown substantially in the past twenty years, produced by scholars of women's studies in China and beyond.[2] Scholarship that transcends national or regional boundaries by focusing on interconnected global processes has grown, including subaltern studies of South Asia and studies of slavery, gender, and sexuality in the Atlantic World. As gender and sexuality have gained prominence in cultural anthropology, sociology, religious studies, and other disciplines that have linked with women's and feminist studies, multidisciplinary approaches to studying histories outside of North America and Europe are increasingly possible. The growing scholarship across regional and disciplinary boundaries makes it hard to keep up with new debates and problems that emerge, but overall the growth of research and increasing transnational compilations provide a wealth of materials and resources.

Combining what you know and what you do not know is a delicate balancing act, which requires matching materials from various regions and organizing them chronologically and/or thematically. Given the vast and growing literature on women, gender, and sexuality in regionally focused subdisciplines, what is the best way to choose topics and materials that will be representative of various regions? Balancing narratives of gender and power alongside comparative lessons that emphasize commonalities as well as differences in the experiences of women across regions and time periods is a major challenge that can be addressed in a number of ways, depending on your goals.

If your course primarily focuses on the experiences of women across the globe, rather than gender dynamics, chronological parallels are more useful than cross-temporal thematic topics, which run the risk of obscuring historical context. For example, comparing the experiences of women across diverse societies in the seventeenth century reveals parallels between the status of unmarried and widowed women in Europe, North America, and Asia. Another common experience that you might want to highlight is slavery across time and space. There are many books on women's experiences as slaves throughout the world, notably two volumes entitled *Women and Slavery*, edited by Gwyn Campbell, Suzanne Miers, and Joseph C. Miller. These collections include a series of essays that reveal commonalities and varied experiences among enslaved women in Africa, the Indian Ocean World, medieval Europe, and the Atlantic World.[3] Simply choosing primary sources or scholarly articles that address similar issues from various regions within a set time period will lend itself to interesting discussions as you compare and contrast the experiences of women around the world. These could include issues ranging from education and labor to marriage and childbirth. In a course that proceeds chronologically, patterns of change and continuity over time will emerge organically.

If your class is focused on gender as an analytical basis for studying world historical patterns and processes, you might choose specific themes and then examine these across national and cultural boundaries. For a course that emphasizes colonialism, race, and nationalism, for example, you could compare the way that gender shapes these in various regional contexts, such as colonial Korea, Ceylon, and Cuba.[4] Structuring a course through these three themes highlights commonalities among women who have similar experiences despite their differing religious, ethnic, and socioeconomic backgrounds, and it exposes structural violence across boundaries. If you choose to explore the role of gender in the construction of ideas about science, medicine, and race in the modern period—an important theme—there are excellent choices for class materials. For example, Philippa Levine's work on disease and medicine in Hong Kong and Southeast Asia can be compared to Rickie Solinger's study of the persistence of biological explanations for single black pregnancy in *Wake Up, Little Susie: Single Pregnancy and Race before Roe v. Wade*.[5] A course that brings together a focus on race, ethnicity, and gender could analyze the history of ideas and knowledge production in various contexts, including colonial

Latin America, the antebellum United States, the British and Japanese empires (including South Africa and Korea), and Nazi Germany.

Teaching about theory from a global perspective can be a bit more tricky. Here, it is imperative to have students first question their own positionality through analyzing their views of present-day constructions of gender and their personal beliefs about sexuality, as we suggested in chapter 4. This will help them recognize that they have a theory of gender and sexuality, and that "theory" is not just something created by cultural commenters and literary critics. You can also help them consider where their theory comes from, that is, what has influenced their own ideas about gender and sexuality. For example, you could discuss the role of biology in contemporary ideas about the basis of sexual orientation. Then you can study the theories of the past and of cultures other than their own, if possible, by analyzing primary documents in their historical context. Exploring the development of ideas about femininity, masculinity, and gender roles across time will allow you to highlight commonalities as well as differences. While it is important to avoid confirming sweeping narratives about the origins of patriarchy, or the inferior status of women in most historical contexts, examining similar ideas of the qualities associated with feminine and masculine behaviors is engaging and leads students to think about global patterns. Plus these are issues that students are generally interested in exploring. Students are likely to recognize that issues of gender and sexuality are politicized today, and that ideas about gender and sexuality are used for political purposes. By starting with their own theories and then moving to those of earlier periods, you can fairly easily explore the ways that ideas were politicized in the past. This will also set up discussions of the ways in which history and tradition are used to make political arguments about gender and sexuality today, which can lead to broader consideration of the political implications of historical arguments on other topics.

In terms of choosing specific materials, it is best to start with what you know. I (Urmi) imagine that most teachers, like me, have a vault of primary source materials that they have found particularly successful in engaging students. These are a good starting point, for if you begin with a few sources that you have already used, you can supplement them with less familiar sources that address similar themes or that provide an alternative perspective on a particular time period.

In order not to overemphasize issues relating to your own regional expertise, construct or modify your syllabus to ensure that you have diversity of scholarship and primary sources. There are numerous databases of primary documents online, available through academic websites that focus on women's history, such as the materials at the Center for History and the New Media (discussed in chapter 2), or regional databases, such as Asia for Educators.[6] If you discover holes in your syllabus (for example, you might realize that you failed to include any content about East Africa or the Caribbean), it might be necessary to go beyond web materials and consult colleagues who work in those regions to find appropriate primary sources or readings.

For example, in teaching about the global impacts of the Industrial Revolution, I have had a lot of success using an anonymous letter written by a widow spinner in Bengal, who wrote to a local newspaper about how she became impoverished due to the introduction of cheap cloth from Britain. Reading this document, along with works by European women who describe the working conditions of young women in England, France, and Germany, provides students with a broader view of the impacts of industrialization on labor conditions in multiple contexts. Contextualizing changes in forms of labor, family structures, and economic conditions opens students to seeing the complex and diverse consequences of the historical processes of colonialism, capitalism, and industrialization.

Another strategy that I have found constructive is using autobiographical texts of individuals who occupy a marginal space in their society. First-person narratives are especially compelling in fostering historical empathy in their readers. For students who have little experience living as an outsider in their own culture, as well as those who can relate to the experience of feeling like an outcast, these perspectives can illuminate theoretical concepts such as intersectionality in a more meaningful way than reading theory alone. If your student body consists mostly of traditional students in their late teens or early twenties, coming-of-age narratives can work particularly well. For example, comparing the experiences of enslaved men and women reveals the limits of race or enslavement alone as a category of analysis. The topics and themes that Olaudah Equiano focuses on in his *Interesting Narrative* compared to those that Harriet Jacobs emphasizes in *Incidents in the Life of a Slave Girl* show how issues of gender and sexuality shaped the lives of enslaved women and men in intense and distinct ways, in terms of the ways that they experienced violence and oppression, as well as the opportunities they had for resistance.[7]

The history of the post–Second World War era of civil rights movements, postcolonialism, and feminism is also rich with the voices of young people. Malcolm X's autobiography provides a decentering perspective on race and identity in the United States.[8] Similarly, Marjane Satrapi's graphic memoir *Persepolis* presents an engaging story that teaches students about the history of the Iranian Revolution, while portraying the complexity of national, religious, and cultural identities through the eyes of a young woman. Satrapi's story naturally lends itself to discussions of the complexity of views about gender, feminism, and sexuality. Because the historical narrative is framed in terms of U.S. and British support for the shah's repressive regime, it leads students to question their preconceptions about the progressivism of Western feminism.[9] Both of these works can be supplemented with excellent documentary films, which are quite moving. My students have responded with historical empathy to the dramatic performances and visual storytelling in Spike Lee's *Malcolm X* (1992) and in the film adaptation of *Persepolis* (2007).

Many of the challenges of globalizing a thematic course are similar to what you would face when globalizing any broad, introductory-level history course, and they depend somewhat on the time period covered by your course. World history courses that focus on the modern period (whether beginning in 1500 or 1750) tend toward a narrative of European colonialism and imperialism, with the rest of the world as marginal territories that enter the narrative as they become colonial spaces. Courses that focus on the era prior to 1500 can become overly regionalized and focused on civilizations, cultures, or world religions, sometimes presenting these in a nonhistorical way with unchanging norms and practices. Courses that attempt to cover the whole of human history can seem overwhelming or confusing to students due to the amount of content and context that is necessary to understand currents of historical change, and they tend toward overly general and broad narratives.

Courses on the history of women, gender, and sexuality have particular versions of these problems. One is the tendency to essentialize or Orientalize cultures outside of the United States and Europe and present them as monolithic and unchanging in terms of gender. For example, studying third genders in Native American cultures could leave students thinking that Native American groups were all more accepting of nonbinary gender roles than were Europeans. Or studies of foot-binding in China could leave students with the impression that premodern China was unique in its maltreatment of women. Thus in the case of studies of third genders, including examples of diverse practices and emphasizing the importance of gendered divisions of labor in most Native American societies would enable students to grapple with the variability in ideas and practices of gender and other issues in Native American society. On foot-binding, a way to avoid the problem would be emphasizing the diversity of popular ideas about gender within China and studying the role of Chinese feminist activists, such as Liang Qichao, who compared the practice of foot-binding to contemporaneous corset-wearing in Western Europe and the United States.

The history of feminism sometimes emerges as a version of the story of Europeans (and Americans) as actors and everyone else as marginal. Students tend to agree that most societies in the "past" had severe gender inequities and that women have historically been second-class citizens in most societies, and they often adhere to a progressive narrative of the rise of feminism and the end of the subjugation of women in their interpretation of the history of the twentieth century. I (Urmi) have found that many young students (who soon will have no memory of the twentieth century) tend to view the post-1960s as a period of progress, in terms of not only women's rights and gender, but also racial equality. When teaching about modern feminism, and the rise of feminist movements, it is difficult to move away from a narrative that portrays the emergence of first-wave feminism in Europe and North America as the precursor to and core influence on movements in the rest of the world. Countering this involves first acknowledging the familiar Western-centric focus in narratives of feminism, then questioning how feminism developed both in connection and in conflict with progressivism and civil rights movements in the twentieth century. It also requires unpacking students' assumptions about feminism, which can be radically different in various regional contexts. In my experience teaching students from northern California to western Kentucky, it is apparent that their ideas about the politics of feminism are very different and affect the way that they relate to "other" cultures.

One strategy that helps in moving away from Western-centric presumptions is to have students read firsthand about women's movements around the globe and how individuals thought about the impacts of feminism.[10] They will find that many of the debates in other parts of the world are quite familiar, such as views about femininity, sexuality, violence, birth control, and women's clothing and fashion, and that numerous issues remain unresolved across cultures. Hyaeweol Choi's collection of documents about women, gender, and sexuality in colonial Korea, for example, is a great resource for analyzing some of the complicated issues that lie at the core of the disconnect between discourses on feminism and imperialism, and at the intersection of feminism and postcolonialism. The volume includes primary documents that illuminate debates about the "new woman" and "modern girl," through which students can explore the ways in which Korean responses to changes in women's roles and gender identity were comparable to Western discourses about women's work and femininity during the era of "flapper" culture in the 1920s.[11] Just as colonial authorities used the language of Western feminism as a justification for colonization, critics of empire focused on the role and behavior of women as a way of protecting cultures from Western/Japanese imperialism and the perceived loss of culture in the face of imperialism.

Similarly, Lila Abu-Lughod's "Do Muslim Women Need Saving?" shows how the American proponents of the War on Terror of the early 2000s justified violence through their discourse on "saving" Afghan women.[12] Highlighting examples such as these exposes patterns that have influenced both contemporary and historical arguments about feminism. They can provoke discussions of the limitations in focusing solely on Western feminism as a universal model, and highlight the necessity of studying the historical and political undercurrents that shape cultural debates on women's rights and gender politics. When I (Merry) teach the women's rights movements, I briefly discuss Susan B. Anthony (1820–1906) in the United States and Sylvia Pankhurst (1882–1960) in England, but to help students understand the international nature of the movement and make comparisons, I have them read sources from Huda Shaarawi (1879–1947), the founder of the Egyptian Feminist Union; Bertha Lutz (1894–1976), the founder of the Federacao Brasileira pelo Progresso Feminino in Brazil; and Hiratsuka Raicho (1886–1972) and Ichikawa Fusae (1893–1981), the founders of the Association of New Women in Japan.[13] In all of these places, feminism was linked with motherhood and nationalism in ways that were both similar and different because of varying cultural contexts and historical circumstances.

In the end, perhaps the best way to approach teaching outside your geographic specialization is to collaborate with scholars who work on other regions. Scholars working within North America or Europe who have experience teaching about other regions and cultures are better equipped to explain these cultures without emphasizing narratives of Western colonialism and empire. If you have focused exclusively on one region in your own work, experiments in co-teaching can be particularly helpful for expanding the scope of your class, as together you and a colleague can provide double the resources in relevant teaching materials, lecture notes, and readings. If co-teaching is not an option, including guest lectures on areas that you are less familiar with is extremely useful, especially in the first iteration of a course. This is also a strategy followed in interdisciplinary women's and gender studies courses, so your students may be familiar with it. I (Urmi) am grateful to numerous colleagues who have given guest lectures in my classes. They have been as instructive to me as they have been to my students, and their suggestions about materials have provided greater depth in my courses.

—— *Chapter Seven* ——

Incorporating Feminist Pedagogy as You Move Online

FEMINIST PRINCIPLES IN A VIRTUAL WORLD

THERE IS A GOOD CHANCE that at some point in your teaching career, you will be asked—or expected—to teach all or part of a course online, as colleges and universities compete to offer online courses and programs. General education requirements and even entire history majors at many universities are now being offered online, and the willingness and ability to teach courses online can also be a clincher for landing a job. This chapter provides guidance for *incorporating feminist pedagogy as you move online*, our seventh design principle. Feminist pedagogy often centers on intensive class discussion and face-to-face interaction. How can this be replicated in an online setting? How can you transform an existing course into one offered online in ways that retain the strengths of the existing course but also take advantage of the online environment? How should readings, responses, discussions, and assignments be modified to create an effective online environment? The suggestions below could also be used in hybrid courses that have both face-to-face (F2F) and online elements, or if you need to move some of your course online because you are traveling during the semester or have a family emergency.[1] They apply to any history course, and most apply to teaching any subject online.

The most important thing to remember is that moving online does not mean you are changing the course content. You are simply switching delivery systems, from one that centers on the voice (yours and your students') and physical presence to one that uses a learning management system (LMS). There are many different brands of LMS, each of which has benefits and detriments, supporters and haters. Universities and colleges choose one over the other because of price, features, administrator preferences, compatibility with other campus technology systems, influential sales pitches, or other reasons. Faculty generally have only a tiny say in this, if any, so you just have to live with whatever your campus has chosen. They all have certain sections: News or Announcements, Content, Discussion, a place for students to turn in assignments (this goes by different names), Grades, and sometimes a few more, such as checklists or quizzes. Our suggestions below are as generic as possible, and should fit with any LMS because they are about *design*, not technology.

A few practical tips before you begin:

- The whole course should be on the LMS when the semester begins, so give yourself plenty of time to plan it.
- Because the LMS varies from campus to campus, and because campuses switch systems, often purge older courses from the LMS, and sometimes claim ownership of anything on their system, you should do as little as possible directly in the system. Instead create and save everything as a separate document, and then upload it. That way you have it, and it is yours.
- Take advantage of workshops, tutorials, courses, and any other help offered by whatever office on your campus runs the LMS. There is often someone there who will look over your course as you are designing it or before it goes live, which can help immensely. She or he can also alert you to new features, changes,

and glitches, and generally make your life as an online instructor easier.

Just as your course content is moving online, so are the ways that you establish and maintain connections with your students and how they connect with one another. Researchers in the field of online learning talk about this as "presence," and they have developed strategies to enhance this and lessen the sense of separation and isolation that both instructors and students often feel when sitting in front of a computer screen instead of walking into a classroom.[2] Presence involves both telepresence (the sense of "being there" in a location remote from one's own immediate setting) and social presence (the sense of "being together with others"). It means creating psychological, emotional, and social, as well as intellectual, connections. Social media does this well, but much online teaching not so well, which is one reason for the very high noncompletion rate in online courses. (Too much time spent on social media is another, but that is not an issue you can control.)

Your creation of a sense of presence begins in the first communication with the students, posted on the News/Announcements section of the course so that they see it immediately and also sent to them as an email message before the course begins. This is your welcome. Make it appealing, meaning—for the LMS version—visual and colorful. Keep using the section regularly for announcements and periodic updates: This week we will be doing x, y, z. Include a to-do list, just as you would announce upcoming due dates, readings, and such orally in an F2F class. And because you want to use every possible opportunity to develop your students' historical thinking skills, do not use the visual material in this section just as illustrations, but discuss these and connect them to the course content. For example, in a week on the early modern period or on female artists, you could use Artemisia Gentileschi's *Judith Slaying Holofernes* (1614–1620) for the News/Announcements page image, which will certainly grab your students' attention with its sword-wielding woman and spurting blood, accompanied by a brief note: "Like male artists, women artists in early modern Europe generally worked on commission for a patron, who hired them to paint specific scenes. Artemisia Gentileschi, the Italian artist who painted the above scene of the biblical heroine Judith cutting off the head of the tyrant Holofernes, was particularly prized for scenes just like this, showing strong women engaged in dramatic actions. This week we will be looking at . . ."

As part of your first News/Announcement message, or as overview material posted via the Content page, you should include some discussion of learning in an online course, as this might be the first time a student has enrolled in one. It is good to be positive about the benefits, but also realistic, as many students think online classes are easier. Here is an example:

> Learning online presents its own rewards and challenges. You will find that the online learning environment allows you to attend class whenever you wish, day or night, seven days a week; you can plan readings and activities around your personal schedule each week. You will be able to respond to the discussion questions at your own pace and then think about how to comment on someone else's responses. Each time you connect with the class you will find that others have responded to your comments and brought up new perspectives and ideas that you have not thought about. This course requires you to stay on top of the readings, discussions, and writing assignments. Its freedom and flexibility means that good time management and individual initiative are of the utmost importance. Some students find it helpful to log on every day, or at least five days a week, and work on the course in smaller amounts of time. If you do not participate actively and consistently, you will not do well.

Your campus office overseeing the LMS often has general guides to netiquette and study strategies to which you can link to augment this, along with tutorials for students about tech issues. You should also have a place on the site where students can ask you a question at any time during the course about technology, the syllabus, or anything course related that they need help with or do not understand, as being able to "talk" directly to you is part of establishing telepresence. This does not mean that you have to be available 24/7; set a time each day (or each day during the work week) that you will answer questions, and let students know when it is.

Creating a sense of social presence, that students are in a class together with others, should also start in the first week with introductions and possibly icebreaker activities. You might want to have students do two introductions: one only for you (posted wherever assignments are posted) and one shared with the other students, posted in the Discussion section. This too can have a historical point, as your response to the Discussion posts can ask students to think about how they shaped their introduction statement, knowing that other students would be reading it, thus getting them to consider purpose, audience, perspective, and so forth in a digital historical source, which is what these are. This can build into a more extensive discussion about historical sources and their limits: What would someone know about your university or city or about students in the early twenty-first century if these introductions were their only source? What would they get wrong? What would future scholars need in order to be able to use these as sources? (Machines that can read them, the ability to decipher the letters, knowledge of the language, and so on.) And it can build into a quick lesson on intersectionality, as the introductions will no doubt involve categories of identity that you will want students to think about throughout the course, such as gender, race, age, marital status, location, sexuality identity, and so on. You could even touch on the concept of marked and unmarked categories, as students' introductions tend to focus on aspects of themselves in which they feel different from most other students: "I am a non-traditional student," "I was born in Laos," "I am a single mom," "I am African American."

To maintain this sense of social presence throughout the course, you can offer opportunities for students to connect with one another regularly through features on the course website, such as a place to share resources relating to course material they have found or answer tech questions for one another, or a place to share jokes, informal personal accounts, or information not related to the course. They might use these, and they might not, just as F2F classes sometimes gel as a group and sometimes do not, but they can be part of your strategy to help students stay engaged and complete the course.

The Content section of the course site is where you post whatever you want students to read, look at, listen to, link to, and so on. Post your syllabus here, so that students have all assignments in one document that they can download and print out, but you should also post readings and assignments by week or by module. If you want to include your own video-taped lectures, PowerPoints with voice-over, or other materials you have made yourself, here is the place for them. As with anything online, these should be short: five minutes tops. Think YouTube, not a conference paper. If you have something complex you want to explain orally, break it up. In an online course, students will hear less of you than they would in a classroom, but conversely the web offers a huge range of materials that would be difficult to use in a classroom: online museum exhibitions students can go through at their own pace and return to again and again, interviews, TED talks, movies and television programs that students can download for a nominal fee (or for no extra charge if they have a Netflix or similar account), and websites with original sources and interpretations. In chapter 4 we talked about using visual materials, and the online environment allows even more of this. The Roy Rosenzweig Center for History and New Media at George Mason University is a great place to start, with lots of primary sources introduced by specialists, reviews of websites, and other materials. They have a general world history resource center, along with ones specifically on women in world history and children and youth in history (see http://worldhistorymatters.org).

The Discussion section of the course is the classroom. Here is where students respond to the readings and other course materials, and then comment on the responses of other students. Everything you post in the Content section should require some type of response from the students, either a Discussion post or an assignment, or both. Students should be required to post a certain number of responses to the materials per week (say, two), and to comment on other students' responses or comments a certain number of times (say, three times). In your weekly assignments for the course, along with readings and other materials, you can include specific questions you want students to answer or topics you want them to discuss in their responses, or leave this more open. And you can add other parameters, such as requiring students to quote from materials to support their views and ideas. You will grade these according to whatever you think is important, including quality of content, number of good postings, amount of interaction with other students, timeliness, and so on.

As in F2F classes, you should take part in these discussions, post your own comments throughout the week, answer questions, pose questions, and help the conversation get back on track if it veers off toward side issues. If you post a long comment or answer to a question or a student posts something that is especially good, copy these and save them on your document record of the course, as they may come in handy the next time you teach the course.

Because you require students to post if they want to pass the course, it is impossible for them to remain silent the way they could in an F2F class. Students who are shy or who want time to reflect before they respond to another student thus have more opportunity to open up. Class dominators can still post more often and at greater length than others, but the rest of the class can ignore their posts or scan them quickly if they do not find them worthwhile rather than having to sit through them. And typing posts takes time, so the balance in contributions by class members is more even than it is in F2F classes, a good fit with feminist pedagogy, in which we want to make the class one that encourages collaborative and reflective communication so that all voices are heard. If your class is large, you can break up the class into smaller groups of five to ten, which can further even things out and give everyone more opportunity to discuss. These can have a discussion leader or a "reporter" in charge of summarizing the discussion, just as small-group discussions in an F2F course often do. Or you could have a general discussion to which everyone must post a response and comments, and then small groups for certain tasks.

Although the course is asynchronous, in order to allow time for students to post comments, the initial responses cannot all come in at the end of the week. So you should require students to post them by midweek (say, Wednesday), and then the comments by Saturday or Sunday, which means the end of the week is the time for online "conversations." If you think that a synchronous discussion would be helpful at some point in the course, there should be a way to do this through an online chat-room feature.

Along with Discussion postings, you will assess students on assignments and/or exams of various types. Exams can be exactly the same as those you would use in an F2F class, but the technology of the LMS gives you various ways to tweak these to make them more effective learning tools. For example, if you normally have objective multiple-choice or true-false questions on quizzes or exams, you can prepare a bank of these and the LMS will randomly select a certain number and present them to each student taking the test. (It can also set a time limit for doing this.) You could then allow students to take the test over again if they do poorly, knowing that the selection of questions will be different, and set the LMS so that it picks the highest attempt when figuring grades. Similarly, you can prepare a bank of IDs and essay questions, and the LMS will randomly select however many that you want students to choose from in their exams. The questions can be posted on the course website at the beginning of the course, just as you might distribute questions in advance for review sessions in an F2F class. Some instructors might feel this is giving too much away, but in our opinion there is ultimately little difference in students learning material because they *think* it will be on the exam or because they *know* it will be. (See chapter 9 for more about this.)

Written assignments also do not have to change, but you might want to develop some that reflect the online environment or take advantage of certain features of an online course. Student research could result in a Wikipedia-style article instead of a traditional research paper, or it could even result in an actual Wikipedia article. WikiProject Women's History is currently trying to improve Wikipedia's coverage of women from a historical perspective, and it welcomes new members, as does WikiProject Gender Studies and WikiProject Feminism. (See the articles on these projects on Wikipedia.) Written assignments could be structured to require students to pull in information or themes from Discussion postings, as these remain on the site for them to read over. In every course we hope that students will incorporate things they have learned in class discussion in their work, but this happens too rarely; assignments in online courses can mandate this. Students can share written work easily with each other through the course website and also can be assigned to comment on the written work of other students in a process of peer review. Feminist pedagogy calls for empowering students, decentering authority in the classroom, and encouraging collaboration; requiring them to respond to the work of other students with an eye to suggesting improvements, and then to take these suggestions seriously for their own work, fits with all these aims.

Beyond written assignments, students could make artifacts that combine image and text, such as a broadsheet describing a witch trial, or a poster appealing to gendered ideas of patriotism. They could assemble a group of objects or images on a topic, similar to a Pinterest site, and then provide a rationale for these choices. They could create a paper or digital zine, those short, handmade, and self-published booklets that were part of 1990s third-wave feminism and have emerged again in feminist and alternative communities.[3] Reports from small-group discussion leaders can be posted as videos instead of in writing, or students could be required to post a short video in response to some of the readings instead of writing a reaction paper. (Your campus LMS office, and most likely some of your students, can provide guidance on how to do this; posting videos shot with a cell phone, tablet, or laptop as "unlisted" videos on YouTube is often the easiest method.) Students are often worried about assignments that include something artistic—wait, you want us to be creative in a history class?—so reassure them that you are not grading these on technique, but on intellectual engagement with the issues, content and use of information, quality of analysis, significance, and originality, just as you do written work. Like written work, these visual and digital assignments can be shared and evaluated through peer review.

Each of these assignments can be launchpads for broader discussions of substantive matters related to the content of the course and of historical method. For example, after students have read about and discussed industrialization, you could ask them to choose four images that they think would best teach students who are not in the class about women's and girls' work in the early twentieth century, and explain why they chose these. This is an assignment that most of them will think is easy, as they choose images and add text about these all the time on social media. So it is your job to complicate this, with questions posted in the Discussion section: What types of work and workplaces showed up in most people's collections? What types of women? What geographic locations? Who, what, and where was left out? Because you have discussed industrialization (and because there are great photographs widely available on the web), there will probably be lots of factory workers and sweatshops in the United States and Europe, and perhaps Japan, but few rural women. So you can use this to initiate a discussion of continuities in work despite great changes, or the chronology of industrialization around the world. Some students might pick images of women working in department stores or as typists, which can lead to discussions of consumer culture and the gendering of certain tasks. Few will probably pick images of women occupied at tasks for which they would not be paid, which can lead to discussions about reproductive labor and the cultural meaning of "work." Students will complain that it is impossible to pick only four to represent *all* women, which can lead to discussion about the choices every historian makes as she chooses evidence and seeks representativeness. You could move to questions about the images themselves. Who made them? What was their purpose? What was their original context? How might different groups of people who saw them at the time have understood them? How does this differ from their meaning to us?[4] This can help students move beyond viewing images as illustrations to understanding that they are interpretive, and that, like written sources, they have a point of view.

This assignment could be used in any course, but if you are teaching online you might use it as the basis of a discussion of historical methods in the digital age as well as course content. For example, in the 1980s women in Latin America led public protests against the actions of military dictatorships; the most famous of these, the Mothers of the Plaza de Mayo in Argentina, gathered weekly, wearing white headscarves embroidered with the names of those whom the government had arrested or secretly executed—the "disappeared"—and painting their silhouettes on walls.

Images of the Mothers of the Plaza de Mayo appear on many websites, in part because they are visually arresting. Thus as you use them to talk about women's political activism in the late twentieth century, you can also pose questions about online research. Start with the image: Where did it appear? ("On the web" is not a sufficient answer.) What was the context and purpose of the image on the website? Then move to the website itself: Who or what entity made it? What are their credentials? Why was it put up? Are there footnotes or links that document the information presented? These are questions essential to good historical practice as students locate, evaluate, and use information, and also to broader digital literacy, for we hope they ask the same questions every time they look at any website. Young people's—and others'—inability to distinguish between real and fake news became a hot topic in the 2016 U.S. presidential campaign and its aftermath, discussed by academics such as Stanford University's Sam Wineburg as well as *Teen Vogue* and other magazines and blogs for young people. Fake news will not be going away, so we will need to add recognizing it to the many other goals we have for our courses.

Teaching online, like learning online, offers rewards and challenges. Some of these come from the situation through which the course is offered. Many for-profit universities and some not-for-profit colleges and universities have created standardized online courses and simply hire people to teach them, often at abysmal pay levels. Students are not well prepared or interested, and many more drop or disappear than in F2F classes. In this situation, it may be hard for you to stay motivated as well. Some instructors who have tried online teaching have decided it is not for them, because interacting with students in person is too big a part of what makes teaching rewarding. We hope that the suggestions in this chapter will be helpful if you do decide to give this a try, for good design is even *more* important in online courses, as your winning personality and sunny smile will not be able to make up for courses that have not been carefully thought through.

—— PART III ——

Common Challenges and Opportunities

IN PART III, we discuss challenges and opportunities that arise when teaching about women, gender, and sexuality in world history, and to some degree when teaching *any* course. We set out three design principles: *fostering historical empathy* to help students understand different ethical frameworks in their historical context; *developing assessments that fit your course goals*; and *connecting with the community* to link your classroom with the wider world.

—— *Chapter Eight* ——

Fostering Historical Empathy

ETHICAL FRAMEWORKS
AND CONTEXTUALIZATION

IN A 1990 ARTICLE in *Exemplaria: A Journal of Theory in Medieval and Renaissance Studies*, the medieval historian Barbara Newman discussed the temptation in women's history to make ethical judgments about the past, to, as she put it, "idealize, pity, or blame."[1] Idealization, pity, and blame have also been features of the history of sexuality, and scholars debate the extent to which this has shaped views of the past. For example, did Native Americans value men who did women's tasks, wore women's clothing, and sometimes took the female role in actual or ritualized same-sex relations as "two-spirit" people who linked the male and female spheres, or is this wishful thinking by contemporary gay activists about individuals who were mocked and regarded as social failures? The first step in avoiding ethical judgments about past societies is understanding that people in them had different frames of reference shaped by their historical context, which you can help students do by *fostering historical empathy*, our eighth design principle. This chapter discusses ways of contextualizing controversial topics and approaching the different moral frameworks of the past regarding gender and sexuality in classrooms where students themselves may well have widely diverse ethical and value systems.[2] These are challenges that face every instructor in world history, but courses on women, gender, and sexuality throw them into high relief.

"Historical empathy" is a common phrase today, part of the American Historical Association (AHA) History Discipline Core and many other lists of the skills, knowledge, and habits of mind that students develop in history. This may be a new term for your students, however, so you might want to take a bit of class time at the beginning of the course to discuss it. One way to do this would be to incorporate "empathy" with other emotions and traits as part of a broader discussion of current biological, psychological, and medical research about the role of brain structure, neural mechanisms, genes, prenatal hormones, and brain chemistry in determining gender, gender identity, and sexual orientation.[3] This is often shortened to "nature vs. nurture." Are men "naturally" better at math or more violent, or is this simply social conditioning? Is there a "gay gene" or a "gay brain," or is same-sex attraction a matter of culture and choice? Research on the brain and body chemistry is extensive, sometimes conflicting, and ongoing, but the extent to which one thinks the brain determines human behavior shapes how one evaluates the different frames of reference of past (and present) societies.

You will not have time for every aspect of the biology/culture relationship, but empathy is, in fact, a good topic to use as an example.[4] Women are widely viewed as having more empathy than men, which is usually ascribed to socialization into female gender roles, but gender differences in empathy are measurable through functional magnetic resonance imaging technology and other methods of testing neurological response, as well as through observing behavior. There are quantitative gender differences in the neural networks involved in cognitive and emotional empathy, evident at birth in infants as well as adults, and in nonhuman animals, so they have roots in biology and cannot simply be cultural. Researchers speculate that this difference might have developed because throughout human evolution (and the evolution of some animals), females were likely the primary caretakers of children, which might have led to an evolutionary neurological adaptation for women to be more aware and responsive to nonverbal expressions and the emotions of others. This included their own children, but also others in the group in which they lived. Because the period when human infants are dependent on others is so long, mothers with good social networks to assist them, developed through empathy, were more likely to have children who survived.

The idea that there is some sort of "maternal instinct" in female human brains is controversial, to say the least, but as neurologists have studied and debated this, evolutionary biologists, anthropologists, historians, and others have begun to study its extension across generations, trying to determine whether grandmothers have had a measurable role in increasing their families' biological success. If they did, this could account for women's long postmenopausal life span, which in a Darwinian evolutionary perspective is otherwise hard to explain. Sarah Hrdy, for example, argues that empathy and cooperation in child care among a large group, rather than competition, better explains how humans became the most successful primate, as selection pressures favored groups as well as individuals that were better able to decode the mental and emotional states of others and to develop strong multigenerational social bonds.[5] Essays in *Grandmotherhood: The Evolutionary Significance of the Second Half of Female Life* analyze the role of grandmothers in prehistoric, historic, and contemporary human societies, and these works would be good to assign to your students both for their content and as an example of how different disciplines can offer ways of coming to better understand the past.[6]

Neurologists and other scientists recognize that empathy, like other traits, is a product not simply of brain chemistry, but of development after birth as well. In fact, one of the key threads in current brain science is the interpenetration of nature and nurture and the difficulty of disentangling these. Thus just as math skills are teachable, so is empathy, particularly empathy for people of the past, a trait that may not have much evolutionary significance the way that empathy for members of one's own group does, but that is essential for historians.

Historical empathy means trying to comprehend what someone experienced from within that person's frame of reference, that is, considering the thoughts, beliefs, and states of mind of past actors. These are even more difficult to discern than actions, and some postmodern historians assert that, because of this, historical empathy is impossible and the only minds that matter are those of the historians who create "history" out of an unknowable past.[7] Trying to understand the ideas and feelings of people long (or not so long) dead does require historical imagination, mentally re-creating what it was like to be in their position. The word "imagination" makes many of us uneasy, however, as it seems to turn us into novelists with no limits on what we propose about the past.

An excellent consideration of this issue, easily understandable to upper-level students, is the lively debate between Natalie Zemon Davis and Robert Finlay about Davis's use of historical imagination and empathy in her portrayal of the individuals involved in the case of Martin Guerre.[8] In her short book *The Return of Martin Guerre*—which became a movie, and is wonderful class material—Davis tells the story of Martin Guerre, a French peasant at the center of a case of imposture.[9] Several years after he had left his wife, child, and village, a man claiming to be Guerre reappeared, and lived with Guerre's wife, Bertrande de Rols, for three years. Conflicts with family members led him to be suspected of impersonation, and he was tried and executed. Davis tries to understand the motivations of all the actors in this fascinating story, including Bertrande de Rols, by using the two contemporary records of the case written by a law clerk and one of the judges, as well as her own deep knowledge of sixteenth-century French village society. (Bertrande herself left no written records, though she may have been able to read.) Davis suggests that Bertrande had most likely collaborated with the imposter, in part because as an abandoned wife she had little status in the community, and she realistically recognized that her husband's return restored her womanly honor and made her daily existence much easier. Finlay criticizes Davis for transforming Bertrande into a "heroic" "proto-feminist" and says that instead Bertrande (and by implication Davis) had been duped by the imposter. Davis responds by reiterating her evidence from the sources about the case, as well as other sources and secondary works about the values and habits of early modern French peasants and early modern women, and wonders why Finlay is unwilling to grant lower-status people the same range of ideas, emotions, and motivations that he does the educated elite Venetian men in his own work. She ends with a consideration of identity and masks, and the ways the boundary between the internal and external self might have been different in the sixteenth century than today, which makes this exchange useful reading for discussions about performativity and layers of identity, as well as historical imagination and method. The AHA links "acceptance of the provisional nature of knowledge" to historical empathy, and this exchange speaks to that as well; Finlay makes categorical statements ("there is no doubt . . ."), whereas Davis is comfortable with conjecture and possibility. Like scientists studying the brain today, she presents evidence as well as hypotheses, though she recognizes that further research may overturn these.

Even the most straightforward narrative of events requires some amount of historical imagination. For example, in his history of Rebecca Protten, a former slave who became a preacher within the Moravian Church of pious Protestants, Jon Sensbach relates that she and her first husband sailed from the Caribbean to Europe. They left the Danish island colony of St. Thomas on November 15, 1741, stopped in the Dutch colony of St. Eustatius for several months, arrived in Amsterdam on April 29, 1742, and then headed for the Moravian settlement at Marienborn in Germany.[10] In describing their leaving St. Thomas, Sensbach utilizes his knowledge about ships and ocean travel and his imagination to give life to the narrative, noting that "the wind carried them out of the harbor," though he has no source that says this explicitly.[11] Similarly, even if we do not know much about this period, we can imagine Rebecca in an intermediate position on a boat crossing the Atlantic, a mental representation that is (and must be, given the physical limits on the human body and the modes of moving it available in the eighteenth century) historically real.

Sensbach uses his knowledge of land travel to imagine a later stage of the trip ("their wagon rattled on into the German countryside"), and then returns to a narrative based more explicitly on specific sources when he relates that Rebecca's husband became sick and died in a small German village on the way. One of the other Moravian missionaries traveling with them described the deathbed scene in great detail in his account of the journey written several months later, including words spoken by Rebecca as she tried to console her husband: "his wife answered that he should not admit such thoughts, or doubt his belief in the Savior, who began this journey with us and would see it through, and that though his body was weak the Savior would give him strength." Rebecca herself left no account of this journey, but a few later letters from her to her second husband have survived, including a testimonial to Jesus, which, combined with writings by others describing her words and actions, allow Sensbach to speculate about what she might have been thinking and feeling at this point, and about her character more generally: "The conviction that she had a divine destiny . . . stayed with her for life." Throughout the book he also highlights the limits of speculation, however, using qualifiers and conditional words (perhaps, most likely, might, could) and making comments such as "her thoughts as the wind carried them out of the harbor *can only be imagined*." This sensitivity to the limits of the knowable is also evident in many other studies of women, which must rely almost always on far less direct evidence than those of men, and in studies of sexuality, which in many times and places is rarely discussed openly. Thus though every history course should help students think about how we know what we know, noting the limits and the point of view of the sources is especially important in those on women/gender/sexuality.[12]

A major part of historical imagination, and thus of historical empathy, is contextualization, that is, showing empathy toward people in the context of their distinctive historical moment. The limits of this are also debatable, however, and your students may have very strong opinions, feeling that any explanation of behavior, words, or actions they find objectionable is a justification, and that trying to develop empathy with people who did or said certain things is itself morally wrong. There is no easy solution to this. It might help to explain from the beginning of the course—and then repeat often—that historical empathy is not the same as sympathy, but is simply seeking to *understand* why people did what they did, not condone it. It might also help if you can present a more complex and broader picture of the people on whom you focus, so that students cannot easily lump them into Newman's idealize, pity, or blame categories. For example, Rebecca Protten is someone whom most contemporary students find easy to idealize: Stolen from home at age six or seven and sold at a slave market, she spoke at least four languages, preached publicly (especially to enslaved women), taught people to read, was imprisoned by colonial authorities as a subversive, refused to back down, and traveled widely. The Moravians, the pietist Protestant group for which she was a spokesperson and proselytizer, also generally come in for praise, as they provided opportunities for independent women's actions as teachers, preachers, and healers, and they even ordained women, including Protten. As Sensbach also notes, however, Moravian devotion, enthusiastically embraced by Protten, focused on the blood and wounds of Christ, with sermons and hymns about swimming in Christ's blood and crawling inside his "moist and juicy side wound," the hole left by a Roman spear, to lick and taste its "succulent purple flesh." Contextualizing Protten on her own terms requires taking this blood-and-wounds spirituality seriously, though most of your students will likely find it extremely weird and some may even find it repulsive or shameful (as did Protten's non-Moravian contemporaries, and many later Moravians who sought to distance themselves from this aspect of their past).

Contextualizing means examining the specific situation in which certain ideas or practices emerged, but it also means looking more broadly to examine their origins and perhaps compare them with similar developments elsewhere. Thus in this example, you could point to earlier meditations on the wounds of Christ in late medieval Catholic devotion, the central importance of the body and blood of Christ in Christian theology, the role of blood as a force of spiritual power in many religions, and so on. You might even have introduced the symbolic role of blood earlier in the course (when talking about the Maya or the Aztecs, for example), so that when students read about the Moravians they will seem less strange. As you plan your course and choose materials, think about topics for which such long-term contextualization will be helpful. If you decide you want to discuss foot-binding, for example, you might include earlier (and later) examples of body modification, or other practices that made women more attractive candidates in the marriage market because they conformed to cultural ideals for women. If you will be discussing veiling, you can set this up with broader discussions of the covering and uncovering of the body (and its various parts), or the spatial separation of men's and women's spheres.[13] Your point is not that foot-binding is the same as boob jobs, or veiling the same as single-sex monasteries, but that diverse culturally and temporally specific practices were (and are) developed in response to similar concerns.

Along with using broader contextualization to help explain things that are unfamiliar, you can actually use your students' reactions to ideas they find strange (or familiar) to move them to a next step in historical empathy: consideration of their own positionality, what is often termed contextualization of the present. On this, the postmodern emphasis on the active role of the historian in creating history has been valuable, particularly when combined with feminist standpoint theory about the ways knowledge is socially situated.[14] Like other historical thinking skills, recognition of their own position in history is something at which students can become increasingly more sophisticated. So it starts with you sharing the questions you ask yourself, which you hope your students will eventually learn to ask of themselves as they become more self-aware historians: Why did I react to the material as I did? What personal assumptions and values am I (perhaps unconsciously) using to make a judgment about it? What frameworks of meaning am I using for this material? How does the social and cultural context in which I live shape my views on this subject? What do I need to learn more about to better understand this source and its author?

Discussing such questions with the class as a whole can help students recognize that historians as well as sources have a variety of perspectives and cultural frameworks. There may well be students in your class, for example, for whom Moravian blood-and-wounds theology does not seem weird, and they could help the rest of the class better understand it. Such moments of peer-to-peer (or student-to-instructor) teaching are to be cherished and are an important aspect of feminist pedagogy, which emphasizes collaboration, shared experiences, and connecting course materials to the students' own lives, but we do not recommend trying to force them. Turning to lesbian students for the "lesbian perspective" on an issue or to

Jewish students for the "Jewish perspective" both puts them on the spot and encourages the class to think that there is such a thing as *the* lesbian perspective or *the* Jewish perspective, rather than a personal perspective shaped (perhaps) by that individual's sexual orientation or religion. In a world history classroom, there may well be individuals who came from (or whose families came from) the places you are discussing, and it is very tempting to turn to them for comments, especially if this is a part of the world about which you have no direct experience or any graduate training. (And for many of us teaching world history, this includes most of the world.) Resist this temptation. If students volunteer information, this can be wonderful, but it can also contribute to generalized stereotyping, so the same questions about individual positionality need to be posed. Being of Chinese heritage does not automatically give a student insight into Confucianism, just as being of German heritage does not automatically give a student insight into Hitler.

Speaking of Hitler (you did not think we could have a chapter on historical empathy and not mention Hitler, did you?) brings us back to the issue of value judgments. Yes, the primary goal of historical empathy is contextualizing the past on its own terms, but we are living in a world that to some degree the decisions of past actors created, which is an aspect of our positionality. Because part of the job of historians and students of history is to analyze cause-and-effect relations and assess significance, there is no escaping value judgments. But to what extent should we as instructors make our own ethical frameworks clear? On most topics discussed in history courses—including Hitler—we generally do not feel it necessary to explain our position. We do not feel it necessary to say that we view a long, healthy life preferable to a short, pain-ridden one, so access to medical care is seen as "good." We do not feel it necessary to explain that we view genocide or the slave trade as "bad," and we discuss various genocides and slave-trading systems in moral terms, even as we also set them in context. Issues of gender and sexuality are trickier, however. In his brief survey *Gender in World History*, Peter Stearns felt it necessary to comment in the introduction that "evaluations in the book assume that relative equality between the sexes is a 'good' thing, which is a modern and not uncontested value."[15] If you agree, you might wish to make a similar statement on your syllabus, or even use the F-word (feminism) that is implied but not stated in Stearns's comment. Or you may feel that your statement of course goals and your choice of materials, or indeed even the fact that you are teaching a course on women, or gender, or sexuality, already make your feminist principles clear enough, and that an explicit statement would make your course goals difficult to accomplish with some students.[16]

Similarly, as part of your discussion of positionality, you may wish to reveal other aspects of your own identity that may not be evident to your students.[17] (Or if you are teaching online, also make evident those that would be visible if you were in a face-to-face classroom.) Or you might want to make this part of initial classroom introductions. Many women's and gender studies courses today include "preferred pronouns" in such introductions, so that trans students or others who present in ways that might be read incorrectly by others can make this known. As with every issue in this book, you will need to decide what to do about this based on what you want to achieve in the course and on the context in which you are teaching.

No matter what you state on the syllabus, your ethical framework will be evident in how you guide discussion as well as lay out the course, though because you are dealing with students who are often developing their own moral frameworks (or questioning the ones they grew up in) and at times with controversial topics, you can never fully control what happens in the classroom. Even the most experienced instructors sometimes find themselves in the middle of an emotionally charged situation, with a discussion that careens out of control. Harking back to empathy may help defuse things, as this is a principle students should use in their relations to one another as well as to the materials. And though the concept of a "teaching moment" sometimes seems trite, reflecting on the situation later as a group may be a useful tool in helping everyone involved become more self-aware.

----- *Chapter Nine* -----

Developing Assessments
That Fit Your Course Goals

TESTS, PAPERS, AND ASSIGNMENTS

PUTTING THIS CHAPTER toward the end of this book reflects the way most of us construct courses: We choose a title or are asked to teach an existing course, set out goals and objectives, decide what we want to cover and how we want to organize it, pick materials, start to map out the weekly or daily topics, redo this when we realize we have forgotten about spring break or a holiday or a day we will be gone from campus, add in guest speakers, and so on. Then when we have finished we think about how we want to assess what the students have learned in the course. Will they take exams, write research papers, do projects? Our tests and other forms of assessment are thus often afterthoughts.

They should not be. One of the most important insights to come out of what is often termed the Scholarship on Teaching and Learning (like everything in the field of education, this has an acronym: SoTL) is that of backward design, developed by Grant Wiggins and Jay McTighe and laid out in *Understanding by Design*.[1] Instead of starting with what you want to cover, they advise, start with what you want students to learn, that description of course learning goals at the beginning of the syllabus. The next step should then be *developing assessments that fit your course goals*, our ninth design principle. Looking at your course goals, you should ask, "How will I know they have learned this? What will I accept as evidence of student understanding and proficiency?" Thus in backward design, you plan assessments *before* you map out the course, as everything in the course—the materials, organization, topics, class activities—will then be chosen to give the students the knowledge and skills that will allow them to do well on these assessments and (you hope) develop habits of mind to carry their understanding and skills beyond the course. This chapter provides suggestions for how to do this; its examples come from courses on women, gender, and sexuality in world history, but the method it outlines works for any history course, or actually any course at all. At the end we include a brief reflection on another type of assessment: student evaluations of our courses and of us as instructors.

There are all kinds of books and websites and worksheets available for backward design, but it is really a very simple process. If you are developing a new course, look at your statement of purpose and learning goals. Here is the one we set out at the end of chapter 1:

> In this course, students will examine world historical patterns and processes, with a focus on issues concerning women, gender, and sexuality. They will come to understand how gender and sexuality have been socially and culturally constructed by global historical developments into highly variable and historically changing systems of power relations, and have in turn shaped other events and structures. They will evaluate how gender and sexuality intersect with other forms of identity and systems of power such as class, race, and ethnicity, and how and why the ideas and actions of individuals and groups, as well as cross-cultural interactions, have transformed these over time. Using primary sources that present a variety of perspectives, along with secondary materials, students will develop credible and effective narratives and analyses about gender and sexuality in the past

that show understanding of the contexts of different historical eras and cultures.

In backward design, you move right from this to determining the types of assessments that will allow you to measure whether students have met these goals. Once you have decided that, you then move to what types of materials and activities you will need to include in the course that will enable them to succeed. We do this below, using the statement above as an example. As is often the case in statements or lists of course goals, the more explicit goals are toward the end, so we work backward.

1. *Students will develop credible and effective narratives and analyses about gender and sexuality in the past that show understanding of the contexts of different historical eras and cultures.* One or more of the course assessments will need to give students the opportunity to write narratives and analyses, or present these orally or digitally. In order to show an understanding of contexts, assignments will need to be fairly long, as historical context is hard to talk about in a meaningful way in just a sentence or two. Turning from assessment to class activities and materials, for students to develop their own credible and effective analyses, students will need examples of these, and you will need to explain why they are good models. That is, you cannot just have them read articles or book chapters to find out what happened (which is the way most students read history); you need to talk with them explicitly about what makes these works credible and effective as historical writing. What sources did the author use? How do they support her argument? What limitations are there in the evidence used? How did the author make her argument persuasive, that is, how does the organization of material and the writing contribute to the quality of the article? You might want to spend some time explaining the difference between narrative and analysis, and provide examples. If you do not, you cannot expect students to know that good history goes beyond "Indira Gandhi was born in 1917 and died in 1974," but instead makes a point about her life.

2. *Students will use primary sources that present a variety of perspectives, along with secondary materials.* One or more of the course assessments will

need to require that students use primary sources, and enough of these to present a variety of perspectives. These assessments should probably require students to compare sources, as that will allow them to tease out different points of view, which is why you want them to have that variety. This means, of course, that your course materials will include primary sources and that you will discuss these in class to help students understand and contextualize them, and/or provide materials that do this, such as readers or websites that have good documentation. You may also want to discuss why it is important to have a variety of perspectives on a topic. Most students will think of this as a matter of fairness ("everyone has their own opinion"), rather than of good historical practice. World history draws on many different types of sources, so you may want to include some that are not written documents, such as artistic works, objects, oral accounts, landscapes that humans have modified, or even materials contained within the human body, such as DNA. Because the vast majority of written sources, particularly from the distant past, were produced by men, nonwritten sources are particularly important in a course on women and gender. Your discussion of primary sources can also move out to secondary materials as you analyze the relationship between historical sources and the secondary interpretations made from them.

3. *Students will evaluate how gender and sexuality intersect with other forms of identity and systems of power such as class, race, and ethnicity.* One or more of the course assessments will need to require students to focus on differences among women or other groups marked by gender or sexuality, and on the ways other social hierarchies have intersected with gender and sexuality in systems of power and domination. Depending on the level of the course, you may want students to demonstrate that they understand intersectionality, the concept that the nature of oppression is multiplicative rather than additive. Thus in choosing materials, you will need to include those that address multiple lines of difference, whatever is appropriate for the period and culture you are studying: race, class, ethnicity, economic status, nationality, religion, language, ability, sexual orientation, age, location, and so on. If intersectionality is a concept you want to be sure students really understand rather than just use as a buzzword,

you will need to thread concepts of otherness, hierarchy, and hegemony throughout the course, rather than having separate units on groups that are somehow "other." You might want to start with examples where difference is very obvious, such as the lives of noblewomen and peasants, then move into more complex ones, or let your students develop those they think matter in the period and place you are studying, which can help reinforce your point that categories are socially constructed and variable. You may also want to address the whole questioning of categories that has come out of queer theory, and have your students consider hybridity, blending, and performance.

4. *Students will evaluate how and why the ideas and actions of individuals and groups have transformed gender and sexuality over time.* Here is where the course goals move into the heart of history: understanding and evaluating change and continuity over time. Although it may seem self-evident, one or more of the course assessments will need to require students to focus on just this, that is, not simply describe some aspect of gender or sexuality "back then" but discuss and analyze change. They will also need to demonstrate they know something about the individuals and groups who brought this change about—or worked against it—which you can do through short answer tests, IDs, quizzes, very brief in-class writing assignments, and similar short assessments. (For those of you who have been worried about how to make sure students know facts as well as have some skills, here is the opportunity.) Even IDs and very short assignments should require students to go beyond knowing who a person was, however, to knowing something about her significance. That needs to be reflected in the points you assign for the IDs on exams, and you need to provide models for how to do this before students take an exam. You may want to provide students with a list of every individual and group—along with events and developments—that might show up on an exam at the beginning of the course, or on review sheets distributed before the exam, which can guide their reviewing (or reading the material in the first place). Some instructors might feel this is giving away too much, but, as we mentioned earlier, whether students learn information because they expect it will be on an exam or because they know it will is not a significant

difference, in our opinion. To allow students to succeed at this goal, you will have to discuss the ideas and actions of individuals and groups, but it is hard to imagine any course that does not do this already. And because you are teaching this now as opposed to decades ago, you will not present these as a series of heroic "women worthies," but ask students to consider possible limitations on human agency in all the systems of power you are already discussing.

5. *Students will evaluate how and why cross-cultural interactions have transformed gender and sexuality over time.* So far this discussion of course goals and the assessments that come from them could apply to any course in the history of women, gender, or sexuality, but here is a goal that reflects the centrality of cross-cultural interactions to world history. Thus one or more of the course assessments will need to focus on significant examples, as well as the processes that led to these interactions, including migration, trade, war, and colonization. Cross-cultural interactions are probably too complex to cover through IDs, but they work quite well for essay exams or short papers. For example, you might ask your students to analyze how the expansion of the Indian Ocean trading network area altered family structure for some groups in the port cities along the Swahili Coast in the postclassical period, or how the slave trade and plantation economy transformed the gender division of labor on all sides of the Atlantic in the early modern period, or how steamship travel across the Pacific created new homosocial (and sometimes homosexual) bonds across class, national, and ethnic lines in the early twentieth century, or how mass communication and cheaper travel in the 1970s facilitated the growth of the international feminist movement.

6. *Students will come to understand how gender and sexuality have been socially and culturally constructed by global historical developments into highly variable and historically changing systems of power relations.* By now in this chapter you know what we will say: One or more of the course assessments will need to give students the opportunity to show they have learned this in a meaningful way, and therefore you need to cover it in the course. But we hardly need to say this, as the impact of global historical developments on the social construction of gender and

sexuality is no doubt the meat of your course. The fact that gender and sexuality are highly variable and historically changing systems of power relations is probably where you start, perhaps by posing the questions "What is gender?" and "What is sexuality" on the very first day. Because you will consider this issue so often, it would be perfect for longer out-of-class research papers and written assignments, in which students explore in more detail how a global historical development that you have talked about briefly in class shaped women's lives, gender structures, or sexual systems. For example, your in-class discussion of resistance to colonialism and the creation of independent nations in Africa after the Second World War may note that women were active in independence movements, but their roles in the new African nations were frequently limited by young male nationalists. Carmen Pereira, an independence leader who fought the Portuguese in Guinea-Bissau in the 1970s, recognized this tendency and noted that women were "fighting two colonialisms"—one of nationalist struggle and one of gender discrimination. Research papers could explore this in different countries and also examine the changes that began in the 1990s, as women became more prominent in formal political processes and as elected leaders, part of a trend toward reform and broader democracy in much of Africa, often led by urban middle-class male and female professionals educated at new universities in their own countries. Research papers are sometimes sniffed at as being old-fashioned, and they are if you just include them in a course without thinking about their purpose and ask students to turn them in the last day. But done well, that is, with preparatory assignments such as topic paragraphs, abstracts, working bibliographies, provisional outlines, and rough drafts turned in for your feedback throughout the semester, they are excellent ways for students to demonstrate that they have, indeed, developed certain habits of mind so that they can take what they are learning in the course and apply it to a new situation.

7. *Students will come to understand how gender and sexuality have in turn shaped other developments and structures.* Here again is a theme for longer essays that analyze what was learned in class or through course readings, or for research papers that apply this to a new situation. You

need to make sure you have talked enough about this point that students grasp it, for textbooks and other materials do not cover this as well as they do the reverse. Discussions of the industrial revolution, for example, generally focus on ways industrialization affected middle- and working-class women in industrializing countries, as middle-class women in Britain and the United States strove to make their homes a "haven in a heartless world" of business and those in Japan to become "good wife, wise mother," while working-class women and girls went into factories or engaged in sweat labor at home. And they may discuss how industrialized cotton production in Britain led to an expansion of slavery and the plantation system across the American South, with hundreds of thousands of people forcibly migrated from the older slave states to the new states of Alabama, Mississippi, and Louisiana, where "King Cotton" ruled, usually with no concern for family relationships. They only rarely discuss ways that existing gender patterns and norms shaped industrialization, however. In both northwestern Europe and Japan, marriage was relatively late, and young women working outside the home in view of men who were not family members was culturally acceptable and fairly common; thus among the many reasons that industrialized textile production took off where it did was a pool of available labor in young unmarried women. So you need to highlight this. The same is true with every religion. Along with discussing how the spread of Buddhism or Islam shaped ideas and structures of gender, for instance, you can explore how existing ideas about women's inferiority, men's military prowess, and the dangers of female sexuality affected (and continue to affect) Buddhist monasticism or social and occupational structures in Muslim-majority countries. Sometimes helping students understand how gender and sexuality shaped other structures can be as simple as making what is invisible visible. For example, from the Neolithic to the nineteenth century, the most common political structure was a hereditary dynasty in which power was handed down through the male line. Thus heterosexual relationships that produced sons (or sometimes children of both sexes) who could legitimately inherit were at the heart of power, which those in power or who hoped to gain it clearly recognized. Every textbook is full of dynasties, from ancient Egypt to contemporary Thailand or Britain, but they rarely mention their gendered (patriarchal), sexualized (heterosexual) nature. Simply pointing this out to students can help them see how intimately gender and sexuality are integrated into structures of political and economic power, even in states that are in theory postdynastic.

At this point you might be saying that what we have just sketched— seven different course goals with various assessments for each of them in only a ten-week quarter or a fifteen-week semester, plus preparatory assignments and discussions of historical method and sources—is impossible. All that class time, all that grading! The trick is to develop assessments that will achieve multiple goals at once. This is moving in the opposite direction to some of the surveillance systems for learning outcomes developed by assessment bureaucrats, in which these are broken down into smaller and smaller "competencies," but it fits with history as a field. Historians develop new understandings of the past by creatively applying all their historical thinking skills at the same time.

Here is an example, from a course on women and gender in the early modern Atlantic World, in which the basic course goals are fairly similar to those listed above. A central activity in the course is reading and discussing original materials from the time period by, for, and about women that capture women's and men's own views of women's lives and notions of gender. Among these are speeches of Queen Elizabeth I of England; the memoirs of Catalina de Erauso, a Spanish nun who put on men's clothing and went to the New World; and extracts from a legal account about Bertrande de Rols, the French peasant we mentioned in chapter 8 whose life is only known to us because her husband, Martin Guerre, left her for many years and his place was taken by an imposter. Students are required to write a ten- to fifteen-page paper in which they imagine that they are one of these women, and they then both *describe* and *explain* their life to the other two. They are instructed to reflect on what these three women shared, and how they differed, both individually and in terms of social class, religion, family situation, geography, and so on. They are allowed to be as creative as they like in terms of format or language as long as the information in the paper is accurate, and they can use information from the secondary readings, class discussion, and the other original sources, along with the readings specifically by or about these women.

This assignment has worked very well, even in a course primarily taken by students who are not history majors. Some students are extremely inventive, turning this into an exchange of letters, a dialogue in which daily life intrudes, a radio play, or a series of blog posts, which in turn have led to rich and unanticipated class discussions on a range of issues. Even the papers that are not especially good fulfill most of the course goals: They are based on original sources (goal 2), grasp that women's lives in the past differed by social class and location (goal 3), show some understanding of the context (goal 1), and recognize that gender was constructed by institutions such as the Catholic Church and the law courts (goal 7). Better papers note that to varying degrees all three women were able to overcome some of the normal limitations on women's actions so may have changed gender ideologies a bit (goal 4), discuss Catalina de Erauso's interactions with men and women in the Spanish colonies (goal 5), and mention that Elizabeth's gender led to her choice not to marry, which determined the course of the English monarchy from that point on (goal 7). Because all three of these women lived at roughly the same time, the assignment does not ask students to focus on change over time very much, but it could be adjusted to compare women across time instead of space. Or if your course focuses on sexuality, it could compare men who had sex with other men (or desired other men) across space or time.

Like any assessment, your grading standards for this should be based on your course goals, the instructions you have given the students for the paper, and the models you have provided and discussed throughout the course. Here is an example of the highest level of standards for this paper, with words from the course goals in italics:

The "A" Range: Your work is superior, well above an average level of competence. This means the following:

1 You consistently show a high level of intellectual engagement with the issues and have clearly thought about the materials to a level that allows you to make your own *credible analysis*.

2 You make *effective* and appropriate use of the information in the *primary sources*, textbook and other *secondary materials*, and class discussion to provide multiple examples and points of emphasis that back up your argument.

3 You present accurate and significant information about *gender* and other social structures and *systems of power*, and about the broader *historical context*.

4 Your paper is coherent and well organized, and your writing is compelling, clear, and *effective* in getting your points across.

The B, C, and D levels for this paper would present the same four categories, with qualifying words and phrases indicating decreasing levels of quality or consistency in quality. B-level papers do what A-level papers do "generally" or "largely" or "sometimes" instead of "consistently," have "some" examples instead of "multiple" ones, and "show some effort" to achieve good organization and writing, but do not always achieve this. C-level papers may not show evidence of much thought about the issue or careful reading of the materials, use sources in a way that is faulty or incomplete, present information that is wrong, and/or have been organized in a way that is hard to follow. D-level papers show more serious problems yet.

As you can see, this list could be used for almost any writing assignment in a history course, with whatever is the primary topic for the course substituted for "gender and other social structures and systems of power" in number 3. If you like—or are required to have—rubrics for grading, you can turn it into a chart and set points for each of the four categories. Or divide or organize them in a different way to emphasize whatever is most important to you in the assignment. However you handle this, it is essential that students have your standards in advance, preferably from the beginning of the course. They need to know how to do well, and this happens only if you tell them. Having clear and explicit grading standards also cuts down on whining about grades, a pleasant side effect.

Backward design assumes you are planning a new course, but what if you already have a syllabus? You can still use the key principle of backward design: Make sure your assessments fit your course goals, and that everything—goals, materials, activities, assessments—is aligned. What is it you want students to know, understand, and be able to do when they have finished the course? Do the assignments and assessments you have designed allow them to demonstrate that they learned this? And have you provided them with guidance on how to do this throughout the course, and explained why it matters?

The assignments that your students produce allow you to assess them as individuals, and they also allow you to judge how well the course has achieved the goals you set for it. Student course evaluations also provide information on this, especially if you are able to create these yourself to fit with your course or construct supplemental evaluations if standard ones must be distributed. You can ask students directly: How well do you think you learned X, Y, or Z? What were the most valuable readings and assignments? What was the most difficult topic to understand? What surprised you most among the things you learned? You need to be prepared for some negative evaluations, for some of what you discuss might make students feel angry, depressed, or defensive, which is not the case for most history courses. (Students just do not get very worked up about the Renaissance or the Meiji Restoration.) If you are including gender and sexuality in a general world history survey, you will get comments that there are too many women and not enough "real" history, though I (Merry) have never had a student tell me a course had too much sex. If you are female, your evaluations and your rating on websites such as *Rate My Professor* will, on average, be lower than those of your male colleagues.[2] Negative evaluations can in turn make us as teachers feel angry, depressed, or defensive, but the positive comments that will be there for your well-designed, distinctive, and challenging course will make up for this.

———— Chapter Ten ————

Connecting with the Community

OPPORTUNITIES FOR LOCAL RESEARCH
AND CIVIC ENGAGEMENT

MANY HISTORY COURSES can take advantage of opportunities for original student research in the local community, but this seems especially appropriate for courses in the history of women, gender, and sexuality or that incorporate significant discussion of these because the push for the inclusion of these topics came in part from outside of academia. This chapter provides suggestions for *connecting with the community*, our tenth design principle. These include research projects that involve the community, as well as ways for students to present their research physically or digitally in public venues or use their knowledge as the basis for experiential learning and civic engagement.

The easiest way logistically to link with the community is to invite someone to visit during class time and talk about their experiences; students are required to be present at this time, so their work or social schedules should not get in the way. Conversations with local activists about their aims and actions, especially those who have long experience with a group, can be a good way for your students to research "how and why the ideas and actions of individuals and groups transformed gender and sexuality over time" (or however you phrased this in your course goals). They can help your students relate the contemporary to earlier time periods, as the guest will no doubt talk about both change and continuity, or your students can be prepped to ask him or her about this. Such conversations can enable students to see how changes were experienced and effected at the local level as well as on the international scene, and they could be enhanced by requiring research into local developments beyond the classroom presentation as part of an assignment. Some college and university libraries also maintain collections of taped interviews with activists, reformers, immigrants, workers, veterans, and others, which can help bring individual actors back on stage and reduce the emphasis on groups that often characterizes courses with a social history emphasis.

In-class presentations and previously recorded interviews can only go so far, so you may want to move beyond this to more extensive oral interviews the students themselves conduct. Research projects could involve having students interview an older family member or acquaintance about a specific issue covered in the course, creating oral histories that can serve as the basis for papers or class discussions. If you include these, you will need to spend some time with the class discussing ethical considerations and practical issues in oral history. The website of the Oral History Association (OHA), the national organization that promotes high-quality oral history, is a good place to start for an overview of these, especially its statement of principles and best practices.[1] This statement emphasizes that "to prepare to ask informed questions, interviewers should conduct background research on the person, topic, and larger context in both primary and secondary sources," a process that can be done with your class as a whole or by students as individuals. If you decide that the whole class will use oral interviews to examine the same issue, you can develop a list of initial questions or topics to serve as a guide together, though recognizing that interviewees—often called "narrators" in oral history—have the right to take the discussion in a direction that addresses their own concerns. They also have the right to see what the interviewer has written and keep a copy.[2] The OHA statement about best practices in oral history contains an eloquent summation that you could use for *all* research in your course (and perhaps include on your syllabus), as it captures the respect for various perspectives and frames of reference that is the heart of historical empathy and feminist methodology:

> All those who use oral history interviews should strive for intellectual honesty and the best application of the skills of their discipline. They should avoid stereotypes, misrepresentations, and manipulations of the narrator's words. This includes foremost striving to retain the integrity of the narrator's perspective, recognizing the subjectivity of the interview, and interpreting and contextualizing the narrative according to the professional standards of the applicable scholarly disciplines.

The interviews should result in some kind of reflective individual assignment, in which students assess and contextualize the interview as they would any other primary source. Because oral history is often eyewitness testimony, students tend to read it transparently as truth (or intentional lying). Thus you need to encourage them to consider how the perspective and social location of the narrator, at both the time of the events recounted and the time of the interview, might have shaped the story told. They should also consider how their own social location—or that of other interviewers if your students are using recorded oral histories—might have affected the interview as well. This does not have to be a long discussion of the complexities of memory, just a reminder that all history is subjective and situated. Oral interviews can also become the basis for small-group projects that reinforce other key themes of the course. For example, because you are probably discussing intersectionality, you might want to have your students group the interviewees by age, ethnic background, sexual orientation, or some other category of identity to see whether meaningful patterns emerge. Or they could start with patterns that *do* emerge, and then see if these track onto categories of identity in ways they expected.

Along with oral presentations and interviews, the written records of local women's groups; LGBTQ and trans organizations; student clubs and associations; civic and religious organizations; community theaters; groups working for gender and/or sexual rights, against sex trafficking, for environmental justice, and on other social justice issues; or other nonprofits also offer possibilities for student research projects that connect with the community. An organization might maintain a file of records and published documents such as newsletters that it would be willing to let students use, especially if those projects are then shared with the organization. If the organization is no longer in existence but was regarded at some point as important, its records might be housed in a university or public archives, and they might even be cataloged. Or archival material might be in boxes in someone's attic or basement, and not cataloged or even organized at all but just jumbled together. Finding a cache of documents held privately is serendipitous, but not uncommon. Even a short run of newsletters from a local group can be instructive for your students, allowing them to see the ways broader developments played out in places with which they are familiar, and sometimes—if they are examining recent history—involving people they might know. Migration, imperialism, industrialization and de-industrialization, warfare, globalization, changes in the gender division of labor, and other major world history topics become less abstract when your students can see their impact right around them. As with oral interviews and class visitors, your students need to do background research to learn about the larger context before they head off to look at documents, and they need to produce some type of reflective analytical piece when they are done.

We have found that research projects on local groups or individuals often make students indignant that the stories they have discovered are not part of the standard narrative. Thus an assignment that builds easily from community research is one that asks them to improve their textbook (or some other narrative) with what they have found. You could ask them to add a paragraph or two that incorporates their findings, thinking about where this would best fit into the existing text. As they do this, they can consider *why* the textbook presents the story as it does, reinforcing your point that history means constructing a past: Was the information they have discovered previously unknown? (Students love to hear they have found something no one knew.) Did the authors of the textbook have a perspective that prevented them from seeing the importance of the individuals or group the students have researched? (On this a common answer from Midwestern students has been: I bet the authors are all from the East Coast, as that is all they talk about.) If what they have found contradicts what the textbook states, you can ask them to think about why this might be so, thus making your point again about the dangers of overgeneralizing about the experiences of gay people, women, or any other group.

It may be difficult within the space of a semester for students to make contacts with a local group, do the research, and produce some type of product, so you may need to make the initial contacts and have a list of individuals and organizations willing to talk with or open their records to students. Sometimes a group may approach *you* or your department seeking someone to help research their history, frequently when they are about to celebrate an anniversary. Whatever the initial connection, you will need to make the purposes of the research clear to the organization: This is part of a history class, not a service-learning project or an internship in women's studies, so what students do has to be related to history. (Though this could include tasks that would be helpful for the group beyond the duration of the project, such as organizing its records.) You and the group may want some type of written memorandum of understanding that spells out what students will do and what they will *not* do, including sharing things on social media without checking first. The organization should receive a copy of whatever the students produce, just as we send our finished research to the archives on which it is based.

Community-based research can result in traditional assignments such as oral presentations or papers, but it also lends itself to experiential learning activities that both actively engage students and appeal to the organization. Students could make posters, artwork, or displays for a meeting or celebration; organize a public forum; re-create a significant event; replicate an object; write and perform a song or short play; or do whatever else their imagination can devise. If performing live seems threatening, they could make videos, short films, or other digital products that can be shared with the organization or posted online, allowing their research to have a longer life. (Permissions issues would need to be negotiated in advance, but this is not insurmountable.) Students need to document the research behind these activities with bibliographies or footnotes, reflect on the process, and analyze the final product just as they would with more traditional assignments, requirements that will help assure them you are not grading them on their artistic or musical ability. Other than the bibliography, however, this documentation could also be digital, as they film the steps in making an object or video-interview one another about their thought process.[3]

Music and theater can offer exceptional ways to link with local organizations on historical topics. As an example, the departments of history, women's and gender studies, peace studies, and theater at several Milwaukee-area colleges and universities have cooperated on four different occasions since 2002 with the Milwaukee Public Theatre and the local chapter of the Women's International League for Peace and Freedom (WILPF) to present *Most Dangerous Women*, a readers' theater musical play. Originally written in 1990 by Jan Maher and Nikki Nojima Louis for the seventy-fifth anniversary of WILPF, the play chronicles women's peace and justice activism around the world from the era of the First World War to the present, primarily through the words of the women themselves. The authors update it nearly every year; the most recent print edition takes the story up to April 2015, and even more recent updates are available from the authors.[4] Public performances have been followed by talk-backs involving local activists of various ages from high school students through senior citizens. Audience members and often the cast members have commented that this is a story completely unknown to them, never taught in history classes (thus inadvertently providing evidence about why women's history courses are still needed). Although a full production would require some funding, as well as a fair amount of time, a read-around in which class members simply sit in a circle and read whatever line comes next is easy to handle and very effective. This could be followed by a panel with local activists currently involved in the issues addressed in the play, or such individuals could even be part of the read-around, most likely adding some generational diversity to your class. Other plays similarly lend themselves to read-arounds, providing your students with an experience of the work closer to what the author intended than if they read it individually and silently.

Oral history and the records of local groups generally privilege the recent past, but experiential learning that connects with community resources does not have to be limited to this. Museum collections and exhibitions offer further opportunities, which may well stretch back into the Paleolithic or at least the classical past with a few Egyptian mummies, Greek vases, and Chinese bronzes, and then more extensive exhibits on area history, however this is defined. They not only provide material objects to study, but also allow you to pose questions of representation, inclusion, point of view, and balance. Visiting these as a class can be difficult logistically, but visiting as an individual once during the semester should not be. Students need to have a specific assignment, although this could be quite simple, say, "Pick five objects in the museum that convey gender relations in the past (or represent historic ideals of femininity and masculinity, or portray sexual or familial relationships, or could be read as somehow queer, or whatever fits with your course objectives), take a picture of these and their labels with your smartphone (with the flash turned off), and be ready to justify your choices."

Museums do not have to be large or fancy to work for an assignment such as this. Athletic or entertainment halls of fame, of which more appear every year, are usually organized historically and lend themselves readily to gender analysis, as do museums that focus on local history or industries. The latter stretch from coast to coast—literally, from the McCurdy Smokehouse Museum on the easternmost point of Maine to the Columbia Memorial Space Center in the former Boeing/Lockheed plant in Los Angeles, where the Apollo command modules were built. Your students might initially wonder how such museums connect with global history, but this should not be too hard for them to tease out. The tiny McCurdy Smokehouse Museum in Lubec, Maine, for example, housed in what was the last operating herring smokehouse in the United States, provides evidence of an industry that once employed thousands of men, women, and children, many of them immigrants, preparing and shipping cases and later cans of smoked herring and sardines around the world in massive quantities. In a building that still smells smoky, the museum displays photographs, tools, and objects of the fishermen who brought in live herring; of the men and boys who killed, brined, strung, drained, dried, and smoked the fish; and of the women and girls who skinned, gutted, boxed, weighed, and shipped the final product. Like many local museums, it celebrates the heritage of this coastal area, but also traces the ways overfishing led to the collapse of fishing stocks, which, along with other transnational economic, environmental, demographic, and cultural changes, brought this way of life to an end.

The rise and fall of extractive industries such as fishing, whaling, fur-trapping, lumbering, and mining is a story that stretches across millennia and around the world, and it is told in hundreds of museums, large and small. Whether the museum labels note its gendered implications or not, the objects will. Extractive industries were (and are) occupations in which the vast majority of the workforce was male, and the workers lived away from their hometowns and villages for extended periods of time in all-male communities, where tasks that were normally done by women, such as cooking and clothing repair, were done by men. These homosocial environments allowed the development of same-sex intimate relations, although these have left little trace in the sources, as the men who engaged in these occupations were generally not literate. They also led to various types of commercial heterosexual relations, sometimes arranged by the companies that ran the industry, which have left more sources and been studied by historians.[5] Sex of any kind is generally not mentioned in local museums, other than perhaps romanticized and coded references to "saloon girls" or "dance-hall women," but your students might well see photographs or objects that provide evidence about sexual relations as well as gender divisions of labor and other types of gendered power.

The photographs your students take of objects in museums can be posted to the course website or a social media page over the semester, and students can be encouraged or required to engage in an online discussion about their own and others' choices. They should also write labels that they think might better identify and explain the objects than the ones currently in the museum, working within the conventions of museum labels to make them short and accessible, and doing further research if necessary. Depending on the circumstances, they could even write to the museum with their suggestions for improvement, thus adding a civic engagement element to their research. Although some museums might not be ready for labels that mention gay fishermen or company-run brothels or lesbian athletes, others will be. Student research projects have led to women's history trails in several cities around the United States, now officially approved and available as smartphone apps.[6] By the end of the semester, the website of photographs, labels, and commentary itself becomes a museum, and a final assignment might be to analyze it. What is there and what is not there? If this course website were your only source for the global history of gender or sexuality, what might you understand and what not? Are the inclusions and exclusions a result of the museums people visited, or the objects they picked? How did this course museum evolve over the semester?

This museum assignment could be done using online museum exhibits, which are often excellent and, of course, easy to access, but we really encourage direct engagement with three-dimensional objects unmediated by a screen or a photographer. Seeing and perhaps even touching the actual object, walking around it, noting its texture, shape, and how it fits into space enhances students' skills of observation and analysis. Objects were created and handled by real people, including those whose lives are otherwise undocumented or underdocumented, which includes most of the people your class is studying. Thus bringing artifacts into the classroom to examine, or assigning your students to do so, can deepen their ideas about how we can learn about the past.[7]

Three-dimensional evidence is generally classified into three types—artifacts, structures, and cultural landscapes—and another way to encourage students to connect with their community is to get them physically out into it. Just as they go to a museum, have them walk through a historic building (sometimes these are also museums), again with specific questions or an assignment. Who lived or worked in different parts of the building? Did this change over time? What objects (food, clothing, household furnishings, raw materials) came in, and where did they come from? If the building was a place of work, what objects went out, who made them, and where did they go? Individual historic buildings have sometimes been preserved, but larger cultural landscapes may now look very different, as buildings have been altered, torn down, or put to other purposes. You could develop an assignment about cultural landscapes using documentary evidence such as city directories or historic maps, but in a course on global history it may be enough just to introduce your students to the *concept* of cultural landscapes, which has been a significant part of history's "spatial turn." They could do this by mapping their own cultural landscape: What spaces do they comfortably inhabit, and how are these shaped by gender, race, class, or other markers of identity? Who controls this, and when and why do these become contested? (Public toilets are often a flashpoint.) Where are the open spaces and community resources, and who benefits from these? What messages about gender and sexuality does their physical environment convey?

We know exactly what you are thinking now, as we have thought it as well: How can I possibly do all this, or even any of it, when I have so much material to cover? This is always a burning question in world history courses, whatever their scope and focus, and a way to answer it is to shift the interrogative from "how" to "why." Even before the current hype about the "flipped classroom," educational research—some of it even quantitative!—has shown that students learn and retain more when they are actively engaged. Activities such as those suggested here are what they will remember, and they might even remember some of the content that you provided as background.

Connecting with the community is also an ethical issue. Oral history was a tool through which women's voices and those of LGBT people entered the historical record, helping to launch both women's and gay history. By interviewing or otherwise researching local developments, your students will continue to bring the experiences of people who have not been part of the past we know to light, a key aim of world history as well.

We view history as a public pursuit, essential to engaged citizenship at the local, national, and global levels, whether it is taught in a classroom, online, through a museum, or around a kitchen table. We hope this primer has provided you with tools and ideas that will help you design and improve courses that promote the kinds of understandings that are crucial to this aim, and that encourage your students to apply their knowledge about gender and sexuality to contemporary issues. We have no doubt they will have plenty of opportunities to do so.

--------- *Notes* ---------

One. Setting Goals

1 This description was written by Merry Wiesner-Hanks, Flannery Burke, and Chauncey Monte-Sano, the three history writers on what became the College, Career, and Civic Life (C3) Framework for Social Studies State Standards, a multistate initiative for improving social studies teaching sponsored by the Council of Chief State School Officers and currently being adopted in various districts and states. National Council for the Social Studies (NCSS), *The College, Career, and Civic Life (C3) Framework for Social Studies State Standards: Guidance for Enhancing the Rigor of K–12 Civics, Economics, Geography, and History* (Silver Spring, MD: NCSS, 2103). Available as a free download at http://www.socialstudies.org/c3.

2 See American Historical Association, "Tuning the History Discipline in the United States," http://www.historians.org/teaching-and-learning/tuning /history-discipline-core.

3 Combahee River Collective, "The Combahee River Collective Statement" (1977), in *Home Girls: A Black Feminist Anthology*, ed. Barbara Smith (Piscataway, NJ: Rutgers University Press, 1983), 264; Kimberlé Crenshaw, "Demarginalizing the Intersection of Race and Sex: A Black Feminist Critique of Antidiscrimination Doctrine, Feminist Theory and Antiracist Politics," *University of Chicago Legal Forum* (1989): 139–166. For recent scholarly discussions of intersectionality, see the special issue of *Signs*, "Intersectionality: Theorizing Power, Empowering Theory," 38(4) (Summer 2013): 785–1055, and, in combination with several other key concepts (crisis, agency, gender binary), in "Forum: Rethinking Key Concepts in Gender History," *Gender and History* 28(2) (August 2016): 299–366.

4 Mohanty's 1986 article, "Under Western Eyes: Feminist Scholarship and Colonial Discourses," became canonical and is reprinted in her *Feminism with-*

out Borders: Decolonizing Theory, Practicing Solidarity (Durham, NC: Duke University Press, 2003), 17–42. Similarly, Spivak's "Can the Subaltern Speak?" in *Marxism and the Interpretation of Culture*, ed. Cary Nelson and Lawrence Grossberg (Urbana-Champaign: University of Illinois Press, 1988), 271–316, has been widely reprinted.

5 Joan Scott, "Gender: A Useful Category of Historical Analysis," *American Historical Review* 91 (1986): 1053–1075, quote on p. 1067. For a discussion of the impact of Scott's work, see *"American Historical Review* Forum: Revisiting 'Gender: A Useful Category of Historical Analysis,'" with articles by Joanne Meyerowitz, Heidi Tinsman, Maria Bucur, Dyan Elliott, Gail Hershatter, and Wang Zheng, and a response by Joan Scott, *American Historical Review*, 113(5) (2008): 1344–1430.

6 A succinct summary of these ideas is Keith Jenkins, *Re-thinking History*, 3rd ed. (London: Routledge, 2003), which was first published in 1991.

7 Denise Riley, *"Am I That Name?": Feminism and the Category of "Women" in History* (Minneapolis: University of Minnesota Press, 1988).

8 Judith Butler, *Gender Trouble: Feminism and the Subversion of Identity*, 2nd ed. (New York: Routledge, 2000); Judith Butler, *Undoing Gender* (London: Routledge, 2004).

9 Anne Fausto-Sterling, *Sexing the Body: Gender Politics and the Construction of Sexuality* (New York: Basic Books, 2000).

10 For a history of the way in which this understanding emerged, see David Valentine, *Imagining Transgender: An Ethnography of a Category* (Durham, NC: Duke University Press, 2007). For key texts and debates, see Susan Stryker and Stephen Whittle, eds., *The Transgender Studies Reader* (London: Routledge, 2006).

11 See Gilbert Herdt, ed., *Third Sex, Third Gender: Beyond Sexual Dimorphism in Culture and History* (New York: Zone, 1994); Sue-Ellen Jacobs, Wesley Thomas, and Sabine Lang, eds., *Two-Spirit People: Native American Gender Identity, Sexuality, and Spirituality* (Urbana-Champaign: University of Illinois Press, 1997); Michael Peletz, *Gender Pluralism: Southeast Asia since Early Modern Times* (London: Routledge, 2009).

12 David L. Eng, Judith Halberstam, and Jose Esteban Munoz, eds., "What's Queer about Queer Studies Now?," special issue, *Social Text* 84–85 (2005).

13 Lynn Hunt, *Writing History in the Global Era* (New York: W. W. Norton, 2015), 39.

14 See Dominic Sachsenmeier, *Global Perspectives on Global History: Theories and Approaches in a Connected World* (Cambridge: Cambridge University Press, 2011).

15 Gayatri Spivak, "Subaltern Studies: Deconstructing Historiography," in *The Spivak Reader: Selected Works of Gayati Chakravorty Spivak*, ed. Donna Landry and Gerald MacLean (London: Routledge, 1995), 214.

16 If you have trouble transforming this into simpler language, or have been taught that complex things require complex words, you might want to look at Randall Munroe's short book, *Thing Explainer: Complicated Stuff in Simple Words* (Boston: Houghton Mifflin, 2015), in which he uses only the thousand (or rather "ten hundred") most common words in English to explain how complex things like the CERN Large Hadron Collider ("big tiny thing hitter") work.

Two. Choosing a Focus and a Title

1 For a solid brief discussion about how to do this in a U.S. women's history course, see Erica L. Ball, "Conceptualizing the Intersectionality of Race, Class, and Gender in U.S. Women's History," in *Clio in the Classroom: A Guide to Teaching U.S. Women's History*, ed. Carol Berkin (New York: Oxford University Press, 2009), 149–161. This collection also has an essay by Mary E. Fredrickson on thinking globally about U.S. women's history, and several others that intersect with issues discussed in this primer.

2 Sarah Shaver Hughes and Brady Hughes's *Women in World History*, vol. 1: *Readings from Prehistory to 1500* (Armonk, NY: M. E. Sharpe, 1995) and *Women in World History*, vol. 2: *Readings from 1500 to the Present* (Armonk, NY: M. E. Sharpe, 1997) are edited collections of secondary materials and primary sources. *Envisioning Women in World History* (New York: McGraw-Hill, 2008) is a two-volume narrative with the break at 1500; the first volume is compiled by Catherine Clay, Chandrika Paul, and Christine Senecal, and the second by Pamela McVay. There are also various popular women's world histories, such as Rosalind Miles's *The Women's History of the World* (New York: HarperCollins, 1989), reissued in 2001 with a snazzier title, *Who Cooked the Last Supper? The Women's History of the World*; or Marilyn French's four-volume *From Eve to Dawn: A History of Women in the World* (New York: Feminist Press at the City University of New York, 2008); timelines of women's history; and inspirational books about great women of the past, but these are rarely used in college classrooms.

3 See http://chnm.gmu.edu/wwh/evidence.php. The general world history website run by CHNM (http://chnm.gmu.edu/worldhistorysources/index.html) also has material on women, and their site *Children and Youth in History* contains material on girls and young women.

4 For an insightful discussion of causation in history and the cultural turn, see R. Bin Wong, "Causation," in *A Concise Companion to History*, ed. Ulinka Rublack (Oxford: Oxford University Press, 2011), 27–56.

5 On Roman Christianity, see Peter Brown, *The Body and Society: Men, Women and Sexual Renunciation in Early Christianity*, 2nd ed. (New York: Columbia University Press, 2008); or Joyce E. Salisbury, *Rome's Christian Empress: Galla Placida Rules at the Twilight of the Empire* (Baltimore, MD: Johns Hopkins University Press, 2015). On China, see Christina Kelley Gilmartin, *Engendering the Chinese Revolution: Radical Women, Communist Politics, and Mass Movements in the 1920s* (Berkeley: University of California Press, 1995); or Susan L. Mann, *Gender and Sexuality in Modern Chinese History* (Cambridge: Cambridge University Press, 2011).

6 Peter Stearns, *Gender in World History*, 2nd ed. (London: Routledge, 2006).

7 Eve Kosofsky Sedgwick, *Epistemology of the Closet* (Durham, NC: Duke University Press, 1993), 44. For a good summary of the idea, and a critique, see David Halperin, "Forgetting Foucault: Acts, Identities, and the History of Sexuality," *Representations* 63 (Summer 1998): 93–120, reprinted in his *How to Do the History of Homosexuality* (Chicago: University of Chicago Press, 2002).

8 Inderpal Grewal and Caren Kaplan, "Global Identities: Theorizing Transnational Studies of Sexuality," *GLQ: A Journal of Gay and Lesbian Studies* 7(4) (2001): 663–679; and "Forum: Transnational Sexualities," *American Historical Review* 114(5) (2009): 1250–1353, with articles by several authors.

9 Susan Lanser, *The Sexuality of History: Modernity and the Sapphic, 1565–1830* (Chicago: University of Chicago Press, 2014), quote on p. 3. The introduction to her book could be used with advanced students interested in how sexuality could have a wider agency. For Foucault in a more global perspective, see Ann Laura Stoler, *Race and the Education of Desire: Foucault's "History of Sexuality" and the Colonial Order of Things* (Durham, NC: Duke University Press, 1995).

10 Matthew Kuefler, *The History of Sexuality Sourcebook* (Toronto: University of Toronto Press, 2007).

11 Ulrike Strasser and Heidi Tinsman, "Engendering World History," *Radical History Review* 91 (Winter 2005): 151–165 and at http://worldhistoryconnected.press.illinois.edu/4.3/strasser.html. This article has a topic-by-topic outline, suggested readings and assignments, commentary on what lectures covered, and discussion of student responses. It appears in a thematic issue of *Radical History Review*, "Two, Three, Many Worlds: Radical Methodologies for Global History," which includes a section "Teaching a Gendered World" that also has an article by me (Merry), "Women's History and World History

Courses" (pp. 133–150), with ideas about how to include gender as a category of analysis in discussions of the European voyages of exploration and early colonialization, as well as an article by Jyotsna Uppal, "Teaching across Borders: Katherine Mayo's *Mother India*" (pp. 165–170), which discusses how to use Mrinalini Sinha's edition of the problematic and polemical *Mother India* (1927) in the classroom.

12 Ulrike Strasser and Heidi Tinsman, "It's a Man's World? World History Meets History of Masculinity, in Latin American Studies for Instance," *Journal of World History* 21(1) (2010): 75–96.

13 Trevor R. Getz and Liz Clarke, *Abina and the Important Men: A Graphic History*, 2nd ed. (New York: Oxford University Press, 2015). The app has an animated movie of Abina's life, along with other resources, and is downloadable for a small fee from https://ebuukuu.com.

14 On the first-wave women's movement, see Leila Rupp, *Worlds of Women: The Making of an International Women's Movement* (Princeton, NJ: Princeton University Press, 1997). On more recent developments, see Chandra Mohanty, Ann Russo, and Lourdes Torres, eds., *Third World Women and the Politics of Feminism* (Bloomington: Indiana University Press, 1991); Bonnie G. Smith, ed., *Global Feminism since 1945* (London: Routledge, 2000); Valentine M. Moghadam, *Globalizing Women: Transnational Feminist Networks* (Baltimore, MD: Johns Hopkins University Press, 2005); and Amrita Basu, ed., *Women's Movements in the Global Era: The Power of Local Feminisms* (Boulder, CO: Westview, 2010).

15 Leila Rupp, *Sapphistries: A Global History of Love between Women* (New York: New York University Press, 2009), provides many examples of female same-sex sexuality across time and space.

Three. Organizing Material

1 Mary Jo Maynes and Ann Waltner, *The Family: A World History* (New York: Oxford University Press, 2012).

2 Peter Stearns, *Sexuality in World History*, 2nd ed. (New York: Routledge, 2017).

3 Jane Slaughter et al., *Sharing the World Stage: Biography and Gender in World History*, 2 vols. (Boston: Cengage, 2008).

4 Bennett's ideas about long-term continuities, what she terms "patriarchal equilibrium," are in many of her writings, including *History Matters: Patriarchy and the Challenge of Feminism* (Philadelphia: University of Pennsylvania Press, 2006).

5 Robert Marks, *The Origins of the Modern World: A Global and Environmen-*

tal Narrative from the Fifteenth to the Twenty-First Century (Lanham, MD: Rowman and Littlefield, 2015).

6 Judith Carney, *In the Shadow of Slavery: Africa's Botanical Legacy in the Atlantic World* (Berkeley: University of California Press, 2011); John Thornton, "Sexual Demography: The Impact of the Slave Trade on Family Structure," in *Women and Slavery in Africa*, ed. Claire C. Robertson and Martin A. Klein (Portsmouth, NH: Heinemann, 1997), 39–47.

7 Robert M. Buffington, Eithne Luibhéid, and Donna J. Guy, eds., *A Global History of Sexuality: The Modern Era* (Oxford: Blackwell, 2014). For a briefer overview that could be used in general world history surveys as well, see Durba Ghosh, "Body Politics, Sexualities, and the 'Modern Family' in Global History," in *World Histories from Below: Disruption and Dissent, 1750 to the Present*, ed. Antoinette Burton and Tony Ballantyne (London: Bloomsbury, 2016), 107–135.

8 Merry E. Wiesner-Hanks, *Gender in History: Global Perspectives*, 2nd ed. (Oxford: Blackwell, 2010).

Four. Incorporating Key Issues

1 Carole R. McCann and Seung-kyung Kim, *Feminist Theory Reader: Local and Global Perspectives* (London: Routledge, 2013).

2 Joan Scott, "Gender: A Useful Category of Historical Analysis," *American Historical Review* 91 (1986): 1053–1075.

3 Jennifer Baumgardner and Amy Richards, *Manifesta: Young Women, Feminism, and the Future* (New York: Farrar, Straus and Giroux, 2000); bell hooks, "Understanding Patriarchy," in *The Will to Change: Men, Masculinity, and Love* (New York: Washington Square Press, 2004).

4 Judith [Jack] Halberstam, *Female Masculinity* (Durham, NC: Duke University Press, 1998); R. W. Connell, "Change among the Gatekeepers: Men, Masculinities, and Gender Equality in the Global Arena," *Signs: Journal of Women in Culture and Society* 30(3) (2005): 1801–1823; Todd Reeser, *Masculinities in Theory: An Introduction* (Oxford: Wiley-Blackwell, 2010).

5 Reeser, *Masculinities in Theory*, 2.

6 Richard Wrangham, *Catching Fire: How Cooking Made Us Human* (New York: Basic Books, 2009).

7 Sabrina Petra Ramet, ed., *Gender Reversals and Gender Cultures: Anthropological and Historical Perspectives* (London: Routledge, 1996); Gilbert Herdt, ed., *Third Sex, Third Gender: Beyond Sexual Dimorphism in Culture and History* (New York: Zone, 1993).

8 Clifton Crais and Pamela Scully, *Sara Baartman and the Hottentot Venus: A Ghost Story and a Biography* (Princeton, NJ: Princeton University Press, 2010).

9 Londa Schiebinger, "Why Mammals Are Called Mammals: Gender Politics in Eighteenth-Century Natural History," *American Historical Review* 98(2) (1993): 382–411; and "Skeletons in the Closet: The First Illustrations of the Female Skeleton in Eighteenth-Century Anatomy," *Representations* 14 (Spring 1986): 42–82.

10 Mrinalini Sinha, "Gender and Nation," in McCann and Kim, *Feminist Theory Reader*; Evelyn Brooks Higginbotham, "African American Women's History and the Metalanguage of Race," *Signs* 17 (1992): 251–274.

11 Lila Abu-Lughod, ed., *Remaking Women: Feminism and Modernity in the Middle East* (Princeton, NJ: Princeton University Press, 1997).

12 "The Discourse of the Veil" is chapter 8 in Ahmed's *Women and Gender in Islam: Historical Roots of a Modern Debate* (New Haven, CT: Yale University Press, 1992). Marjane Satrapi, *The Complete Persepolis* (New York: Pantheon, 2007).

13 Chandra Talpade Mohanty, *Feminism without Borders: Decolonizing Theory, Practicing Solidarity* (Durham, NC: Duke University Press, 2003).

14 Lila Abu-Lughod, "The Romance of Resistance: Tracing Transformations of Power through Bedouin Women," *American Ethnologist* 17 (1990): 41–55.

15 Gayatri Chakravorty Spivak, "Can the Subaltern Speak?," in *Marxism and the Interpretation of Culture*, ed. Cary Nelson and Lawrence Grossberg (Urbana-Champaign: University of Illinois Press, 1988).

16 Nupur Chaudhuri, Sherry J. Katz, and Mary Elizabeth Perry, eds., *Contesting Archives: Finding Women in the Sources* (Urbana-Champaign: University of Illinois Press, 2010).

17 Trevor Burnard, *Mastery, Tyranny, & Desire: Thomas Thistlewood and His Slaves in the Anglo-Jamaican World* (Chapel Hill: University of North Carolina Press, 2004).

18 Cheshire Calhoun, "Separating Lesbian Theory from Feminist Theory," in McCann and Kim, *Feminist Theory Reader*, 396; Charlotte Bunch, "Lesbians in Revolt," in McCann and Kim, *Feminist Theory Reader*, 129.

19 Gayle Rubin, "Thinking Sex: Notes for a Radical Theory of the Politics of Sexuality," in *Pleasure and Danger*, ed. Carole Vance (London: Routledge and Kegan Paul, 1984), 143–178; Eve Kosofsky Sedgwick, *Epistemology of the Closet* (Durham, NC: Duke University Press, 1993). If students want a longer discussion of queer theory, they could read Annamarie Jagose, *Queer Theory: An Introduction* (New York: New York University Press, 1997).

20 George Chauncey, *Gay New York: Gender, Urban Culture, and the Making of the Gay Male World, 1890–1940* (New York: Basic Books, 1995); John D'Emilio and Estelle Friedman, *Intimate Matters: A History of Sexuality in*

America, 3rd ed. (Chicago: University of Chicago Press, 2012); Cindy Patton and Benigno Sánchez-Eppler, eds., *Queer Diasporas* (Durham, NC: Duke University Press, 2000); Sokari Ekine and Hakima Abbas, eds., *Queer African Reader* (Nairobi: Pambazuka Press, 2013).

21 John D'Emilio, "Capitalism and Gay Identity," in *Powers of Desire: The Politics of Sexuality*, ed. Ann Snitow, Christine Stansell, and Sharan Thompson (New York: New Feminist Library Series, 1983), 100–113.

22 Judith Butler, "Performative Acts and Gender Constitution: An Essay in Phenomenology and Feminist Theory," *Theatre Journal* 40(4) (1988): 519–531; Antoinette Burton, *Dwelling in the Archive: Women Writing House, Home, and History in Late Colonial India* (Oxford: Oxford University Press, 2003); Chauncey, *Gay New York*; Ekine and Abbas, *Queer African Reader*.

23 Heidi Hartmann, "The Unhappy Marriage of Marxism and Feminism: Towards a More Progressive Union," *Capital and Class* 3(2) (Summer 1979): 1–33.

24 Edward Said, *Orientalism* (New York: Vintage, 1979); Nell Irvin Painter, *The History of White People* (New York: W. W. Norton, 2011).

25 Sander Gilman, "Black Bodies, White Bodies: Toward an Iconography of Female Sexuality in Late Nineteenth-Century Art, Medicine, and Literature," *Critical Inquiry* 12(1) (1985): 204–242.

26 Djurdja Bartlett, *Fashioneast: The Spectre That Haunted Socialism* (Cambridge, MA: MIT Press, 2010).

27 Thomas L. Kelly and John Frederick, *Fallen Angels: The Sex Workers of South Asia* (New Delhi: Roli Books, 2000).

Five. Integrating Gender More Fully

1 Lin Foxhall, *Studying Gender in Classical Antiquity* (New York: Cambridge University Press, 2013).

2 Dagmar Herzog, "Syncopated Sex: Transforming European Sexual Cultures," *American Historical Review* 114(5) (2009): 1305. This article is part of an *AHR* Forum on transnational sexualities, with articles by different authors that review trends in scholarship on various parts of the world.

3 Thomas Hubbard, *Homosexuality in Greece and Rome: A Sourcebook* (Berkeley: University of California Press, 2003). James N. Davidson's *Courtesans and Fishcakes: The Consuming Passions of Classical Athens* (Chicago: University of Chicago Press, 1997) has fascinating stories about daily life and desire in Athens that you could mine for your course, though it assumes a little too much knowledge to make it accessible to most undergraduates.

4 This point is made in Nirmala S. Sangado, *Buddhist Nuns and Gendered Practice: In Search of the Female Renunciate* (New York: Oxford University Press,

2013), which provides a thoughtful and sophisticated examination of the practices and lives of Buddhist nuns today.

5 Liz Wilson, *Charming Cadavers: Horrific Figurations of the Feminine in Indian Buddhist Hagiographic Literature* (Chicago: University of Chicago Press, 1996).

6 Jonathan Powers, *A Bull of a Man: Images of Masculinity, Sex, and the Body in Indian Buddhism* (Cambridge, MA: Harvard University Press, 2009).

7 Kathleen Wilson, *The Island Race: Englishness, Empire and Gender in the Eighteenth Century* (New York: Routledge, 2003).

8 Zine Magubane, *Bringing the Empire Home: Race, Class, and Gender in Britain and Colonial South Africa* (Chicago: University of Chicago Press, 2004).

9 Julia Clancy-Smith and Frances Gouda, *Race, Gender, and Family Life in French and Dutch Colonialism* (Charlottesville: University Press of Virginia, 1998). For a longer study of French women and colonialism, see Marie-Paule Ha, *French Women and the Empire: The Case of Indochina* (New York: Oxford University Press, 2014).

10 Peggy Pascoe, *What Comes Naturally: Miscegenation Law and the Making of Race in America* (New York: Oxford University Press, 2010).

11 Magal M. Carrera, *Imagining Identity in New Spain: Race, Lineage, and the Colonial Body in Portraiture and Casta Paintings* (Austin: University of Texas Press, 2003).

12 Additional readings for more advanced students include Marilyn Lake and Henry Reynolds, *Drawing the Global Colour Line: White Men's Countries and the International Challenge of Racial Equality* (Cambridge: Cambridge University Press, 2008); and Ann Laura Stoler, *Carnal Knowledge and Imperial Power: Race and the Intimate in Colonial Rule*, 2nd ed. (Berkeley: University of California Press, 2011).

13 Jane E. Mangan, *Transatlantic Obligations: Creating the Bonds of Family in Conquest-Era Peru and Spain* (New York: Oxford University Press, 2016); Tony Ballantyne and Antoinette Burton, eds., *Bodies in Contact: Rethinking Colonial Encounters in World History* (Durham, NC: Duke University Press, 2005).

14 Among the many readings on this are Sabrina Petra Ramet, ed., *Gender Reversals and Gender Cultures: Anthropological and Historical Perspectives* (London: Routledge, 1996); Sue-Ellen Jacobs, Wesley Thomas, and Sabine Lang, eds., *Two-Spirit People: Native American Gender Identity, Sexuality, and Spirituality* (Urbana-Champaign: University of Illinois Press, 1997); Gayatri Reddy, *With Respect to Sex: Negotiating Hijra Identity in South India* (Chicago: University of Chicago Press, 2005); and Susan Stryker, *Transgender History* (Berkeley, CA: Seal Press, 2008).

15 The latter film is available as a free download at http://aplaceinthemiddle.org.

Six. Globalizing a Regionally Based Course

1   Bonnie Smith, ed., *Women's History in Global Perspective*, 3 vols. (Urbana-Champaign: University of Illinois Press, 2004).

2   Gail Hershatter, "State of the Field: Women in China's Long Twentieth Century," *Journal of Asian Studies* 63(4) (2004): 991–1065.

3   Gwyn Campbell, Suzanne Miers, and Joseph C. Miller, eds., *Women and Slavery*, vol. 1: *Africa, the Indian Ocean World, and the Medieval North Atlantic* (Athens: Ohio University Press, 2007); and *Women and Slavery*, vol. 2: *The Modern Atlantic* (Athens: Ohio University Press, 2008).

4   Theodore Jun Yoo, *The Politics of Gender in Colonial Korea: Education, Labor, and Health, 1910–1945* (Berkeley: University of California Press, 2008); Malathi de Alwis, "'Respectability,' 'Modernity,' and the Policing of 'Culture' in Colonial Ceylon," along with other essays in Antoinette Burton, ed., *Gender, Sexuality, and Colonial Modernities* (London: Routledge, 1999); Luis Martinez-Fernandez, "The 'Male City' of Havana: The Coexisting Logics of Colonialism, Slavery, and Patriarchy in Nineteenth-Century Cuba," and other essays in *Women and the Colonial Gaze*, ed. Tamara L. Hunt and Micheline R. Lessard (New York: New York University Press, 2002).

5   Philippa Levine, *Prostitution, Race, and Politics: Policing Venereal Disease in the British Empire* (London: Routledge, 2003); Rickie Solinger, *Wake Up, Little Susie: Single Pregnancy and Race before Roe v. Wade* (London: Routledge, 2000). See also Londa Schiebinger, *Nature's Body: Gender in the Making of Modern Science* (Boston: Beacon, 1993).

6   Asia for Educators, http://afe.easia.columbia.edu/.

7   Olaudah Equiano, *The Interesting Narrative and Other Writings* (New York: Penguin Classics, 2003); Harriet Jacobs, *Incidents in the Life of a Slave Girl* (Boston: Dover Thrift Editions, 2001). There are selections from Equiano's narrative, with a good introduction by Stephen Mintz, at the *Children and Youth in History* website run by the Center for History and New Media: http://chnm.gmu.edu/cyh/case-studies/57. This website also has other excellent primary sources about young people.

8   Malcolm X and Alex Haley, *The Autobiography of Malcolm X as Told to Alex Haley* (New York: Ballantine, 1964).

9   Marjane Satrapi, *The Complete Persepolis* (New York: Pantheon, 2007). For other original sources about young people, see the *Children and Youth in History* website.

10   Leila Rupp, *Worlds of Women: The Making of an International Women's Movement* (Princeton, NJ: Princeton University Press, 1997); Amrita Basu, ed., *Women's Movements in the Global Era: The Power of Local Feminisms* (Boul-

der, CO: Westview, 2010); Valentine M. Moghadam, *Globalizing Women: Transnational Feminist Networks* (Baltimore, MD: Johns Hopkins University Press, 2005); Bonnie G. Smith, ed., *Global Feminism since 1945* (London: Routledge, 2000).

11 Hyaeweol Choi, ed., *New Women in Colonial Korea: A Sourcebook* (London: Routledge, 2013).

12 Lila Abu-Lughod, "Do Muslim Women Really Need Saving? Anthropological Reflections on Cultural Relativism and Its Others," *American Anthropologist* 104(3) (September 2002): 783–790.

13 These sources can be found in "Nationalism, Motherhood, and Women's Rights in Brazil, Egypt, and Japan (1890s–1930s)," in Merry Wiesner et al., *Discovering the Global Past: A Look at the Evidence*, vol. 2, 4th ed. (New York: Cengage, 2011).

Seven. Incorporating Feminist Pedagogy

1 This chapter profited greatly from discussions with Mary Delgado, an online institutional designer at Concordia University Wisconsin, and Linda Cotter, a graduate student in education at the University of Wisconsin–Milwaukee.

2 A brief guide with some theory and lots of practical tips is Rosemary M. Lehman and Simone C. O. Conceiçao, *Creating a Sense of Presence in Online Teaching: How to "Be There" for Distance Learners* (San Francisco: Jossey-Bass, 2010).

3 There is information on feminist zines from around the world at the Grrrl Zine Network, http://www.grrrlzines.net/about.htm. (The site is no longer maintained, but the main pages are still up and many of the links are still good.) Many academic libraries have feminist zine collections that your students can use for examples or research. Among the largest are those at Barnard College and the Sallie Bingham Center for Women's History and Culture at Duke University.

4 There is an excellent introduction to analyzing images in world history by Irene Bierman, "Material Culture/Images," on the *World History Sources* site, which you could include in your assigned course readings: http://chnm.gmu.edu/worldhistorysources/unpacking/imagesmain.html.

Eight. Fostering Historical Empathy

1 Barbara Newman, "On the Ethics of Feminist Historiography," *Exemplaria: A Journal of Theory in Medieval and Renaissance Studies* 2(2) (1990): 702–706, quote on p. 702.

2 This chapter benefited greatly from Stephane Levesque, "How Can We Understand Predecessors Who Had Different Moral Frameworks?—Historical Empathy," in *Thinking Historically: Educating Students for the Twenty-First Century* (Toronto: University of Toronto Press, 2008), 140–169.

3 Two short recent studies are Dick F. Swaab, "Sexual Orientation and Its Basis in Brain Structure and Function," *Proceedings of the National Academy of Sciences* 105(30) (2008): 10273–10274; and Melissa Hines, "Sex-Related Variation in Human Behavior and the Brain," *Trends in Cognitive Sciences* 14(10) (2010): 448–456. Many science blogs, such as that hosted by *Scientific American*, have posts and threads on this issue.

4 There is a good review of evidence from neuroscience, social psychology, behavioral biology, and economics about this, in language fairly accessible to nonscientists, in Leonardo Christov-Moore et al., "Empathy: Gender Effects in Brain and Behavior," *Neuroscience and Biobehavioral Reviews* 46 (2014): 604–627.

5 Sarah Blaffer Hrdy, *Mothers and Others: The Evolutionary Origins of Mutual Understanding* (Cambridge: Belknap, 2009). This is a long book, but you could use parts of it with your students.

6 Eckard Voland, Anthanasios Chasiotis, and Wulf Schiefenhovel, eds., *Grandmotherhood: The Evolutionary Significance of the Second Half of Female Life* (New Brunswick, NJ: Rutgers University Press, 2005).

7 Keith Jenkins, *Re-thinking History*, 3rd ed. (London: Routledge, 2003).

8 Robert Finlay, "The Refashioning of Martin Guerre," *American Historical Review* 93(3) (June 1988): 553–571; and Natalie Zemon Davis, "On the Lame," *American Historical Review* 93(3) (June 1988): 572–603.

9 Natalie Zemon Davis, *The Return of Martin Guerre* (Cambridge, MA: Harvard University Press, 1983).

10 Jon F. Sensbach, *Rebecca's Revival: Creating Black Christianity in the Atlantic World* (Cambridge, MA: Harvard University Press, 2005), 159. This book traces Rebecca Protten's remarkable life and career in the Caribbean, Europe, and West Africa, and is wonderful for courses.

11 Sensbach, *Rebecca's Revival*, 159.

12 Sensbach, *Rebecca's Revival*, 159 (emphasis added), 213. On barriers to knowledge about sex and strategies for addressing these, see Valerie Traub, *Thinking Sex with the Early Moderns* (Philadelphia: University of Pennsylvania Press, 2015). On sources in women's history, see Jo Ann McNamara, "De quibusdam mulieribus: Reading Women's History from Hostile Sources," in *Medieval Women and the Sources of Medieval History*, ed. Joel T. Rosenthal (Athens: University of Georgia Press, 1990), 237–258.

13 For more ideas on this, see Antoinette Burton, "The Body in/as World History," in *A Companion to World History*, ed. Douglas Northrop (Malden, MA: Wiley-Blackwell, 2012), 272–284.

14 See Sandra Harding and Merrill B. Hintikka, eds., *The Feminist Standpoint Theory Reader: Intellectual and Political Controversies* (New York: Routledge, 2004).

15 Peter Stearns, *Gender in World History*, 2nd ed. (London: Routledge, 2006), 8.

16 For an excellent example of how to build up to complex gender concepts with skeptical students, see Jacqueline Z. Wilson, "Don't Mention the 'F' Word: Using Images of Transgressive Texts to Teach Gendered History," in *Feminist Pedagogy in Higher Education: Critical Theory and Practice*, ed. Tracy Penny Light, Jane Nicholas, and Renee Bondy (Waterloo, Ontario: Wilfrid Laurier University Press, 2015), 221–243.

17 For one perspective on this, see Linda McCarty, "Wearing My Identity: A Transgender Teacher in the Classroom," *Equity and Excellence in Education* 36(2) (June 2003): 170–183.

Nine. Developing Assessments

1 Grant Wiggins and Jay McTighe, *Understanding by Design*, 2nd ed. (Alexandria, VA: Association for Supervision and Curricular Development, 2005).

2 Gender disparities in course evaluations have been traced in every field. For a fascinating new tool that allows you to see how the words used to describe male and female teachers compare in about fourteen million reviews, broken down by academic discipline, from *Rate My Professor* (http://www.ratemyprofessor.com), see the *Gender and Teacher Reviews* site, http://benschmidt.org/profGender/#. Male instructors are more often described as good, smart, great, knowledgeable, funny, or brilliant (though also more often as boring), while female instructors are more often described as poor or mean, but also more often as organized, caring, and understanding. Interestingly, out of the twenty-five disciplines listed, history instructors ranked second to last for "caring," with only economics professors beneath us.

Ten. Connecting with the Community

1 See the Oral History Association website at http://www.oralhistory.org/about/principles-and-practices/. There is an excellent short list of practical tips for interviewing, "Oral History Tips," from the University of California at Berkeley at http://www.lib.berkeley.edu/libraries/bancroft-library/oral-history-center/oral-history-tips. Other good websites with interview guidelines, sam-

ple letters for approaching possible interviewees, and forms for informed consent can be found at the Nebraska State Historical Society (http://www
.nebraskahistory.org/lib-arch/research/audiovis/oral_history/), the UCLA
Library Center for Oral History Research (http://oralhistory.library.ucla.edu
/interviewGuidelines.html), and the Center for the Study of History and
Memory at Indiana University (http://www.indiana.edu/%7Ecshm/techniques
.html). On feminist oral history, see Margaret S. Crocco, "Teaching Women's
History through Oral History," in *Clio in the Classroom: A Guide to Teaching
U.S. Women's History*, ed. Carol Berkin (New York: Oxford University Press,
2009), 253–266; and Sherna Berger Gluck and Daphne Patai, eds., *Women's
Words: The Feminist Practice of Oral History* (New York: Routledge, 1991).

2 Since the 1990s, oral history research at many universities has fallen under the
purview of Institutional Review Boards (IRBs), generally made up of scholars
in the biomedical and behavioral sciences, who have different concerns than
historians and have sometimes placed undue restrictions on history research.
Over the last decade, the Office of Human Research Protection at the Department of Health and Human Services has issued new recommendations, and
on January 19, 2017, it "explicitly removed" oral history and journalism from
the Federal Policy for the Protection of Human Subjects, because these "focus
directly on the specific individuals about whom the information is collected"
(https://www.federalregister.gov/documents/2017/01/19/2017-01058/federal
-policy-for-the-protection-of-human-subjects).

The new IRB rule went into effect January 19, 2018. Because campuses may
still consider social science research outside of history to need IRB approval,
check with your local IRB for the rules that apply if you are teaching in a women's and gender studies or other interdisciplinary program.

3 Experiential learning does not have to be limited to community-based research, of course, but could be an option for any assignment. For some short reflections by historians who have introduced this into their classrooms in what
might seem to be a very traditional field, see "Experiential Learning In and
Out of the Classroom," *Sixteenth Century Journal* 46(4) (2015): 1009–1032.

4 Jan Maher, *Most Dangerous Women, Readers' Theatre Edition* (Plattsburgh,
NY: Dog Hollow Press, 2015). This edition contains the entire script, along
with suggestions for how to use the play in classroom and community settings,
topics and discussion questions for extended research, and short biographies
of every person mentioned in the play. If you plan a public performance,
Local Access provides a simple score of the songs upon payment of modest
royalties, and it can also provide updates to the script through March 2017:
localaccess@aol.com.

5 On commercialized sex and extractive industries in the nineteenth and early
   twentieth centuries, see Raelene Frances, "Dealing with the Social Evil: Prostitution and the Police in Perth and on the Eastern Goldfields, 1895–1924,"
   in *So Much Hard Work: Women and Prostitution in Australian History*, ed.
   K. Daniels (Sydney: Fontana, 1984); Jan MacKall, *Brothels, Bordellos, and Bad
   Girls: Prostitution in Colorado, 1860–1930* (Albuquerque: University of New
   Mexico Press, 2004); Joan M. Jensen, *Calling This Place Home: Women on the
   Wisconsin Frontier, 1850–1925* (St. Paul: Minnesota Historical Society, 2006),
   213–217; Jan Jordan, "Of Whalers, Diggers, and 'Soiled Doves': A History of
   the Sex Industry in New Zealand," in *Taking the Crime Out of Sex Work: New
   Zealand Sex Workers Fight for Decriminalisation*, ed. Gilian Abel et al. (Bris-
   tol: Policy Press, 2010), 25–44. For more recent times, see Meredeth Turshen,
   *Gender and the Political Economy of Conflict in Africa: The Persistence of Vio-
   lence* (London: Routledge, 2016).
6 See, for example, the Boston Women's Heritage Trail: http://bwht.org.
7 On this issue, see Anne M. Derousie and Vivien E. Rose, "History You Can
   Touch: Teaching Women's History through Three-Dimensional Objects,"
   in Berkin, *Clio in the Classroom*, 239–252. A good introduction for students,
   with chapters from many parts of the world, is Karen Harvey, ed., *History and
   Material Culture: A Student's Guide to Approaching Alternative Sources* (New
   York: Routledge, 2009).

—— *Selected Bibliography* ——

Textbooks, Surveys, and Collections Designed for Use in the Classroom

Beasley, Chris. *Gender and Sexuality: Critical Theories, Critical Thinkers.* London: Sage, 2005.

Buffington, Robert M., Eithne Luibhéid, and Donna J. Guy, eds. *A Global History of Sexuality: The Modern Era.* Oxford: Blackwell, 2014.

Clay, Catherine, Chandrika Paul, and Christine Senecal. *Envisioning Women in World History*, vol. 1. New York: McGraw-Hill, 2008.

Harding, Sandra, and Merrill B. Hintikka, eds. *The Feminist Standpoint Theory Reader: Intellectual and Political Controversies.* New York: Routledge, 2004.

Hughes, Sarah Shaver, and Brady Hughes, eds. *Women in World History: Readings from 1500 to the Present.* Armonk, NY: M. E. Sharpe, 1997.

Hughes, Sarah Shaver, and Brady Hughes, eds. *Women in World History: Readings from Prehistory to 1500.* Armonk, NY: M. E. Sharpe, 1995.

Jagose, Annamarie. *Queer Theory: An Introduction.* New York: New York University Press, 1997.

Kuefler, Matthew, ed. *The History of Sexuality Sourcebook.* Toronto: University of Toronto Press, 2007.

Maynes, Mary Jo, and Ann Waltner. *The Family: A World History.* New York: Oxford University Press, 2012.

McCann, Carole R., and Seung-kyung Kim, eds. *Feminist Theory Reader: Local and Global Perspectives.* London: Routledge, 2013.

McVay, Pamela. *Envisioning Women in World History*, vol. 2. New York: McGraw-Hill, 2008.

Reeser, Todd. *Masculinities in Theory: An Introduction.* Oxford: Wiley-Blackwell, 2010.

Rupp, Leila. *Sapphistries: A Global History of Love between Women.* New York: New York University Press, 2009.

Slaughter, Jane, et al., eds. *Sharing the World Stage: Biography and Gender in World History*. 2 vols. Boston: Cengage, 2008.

Smith, Bonnie, ed. *Women's History in Global Perspective*. 3 vols. Urbana-Champaign: University of Illinois Press, 2004.

Stearns, Peter. *Gender in World History*. 2nd ed. London: Routledge, 2006.

Stearns, Peter. *Sexuality in World History*. 2nd ed. London: Routledge, 2017.

Stryker, Susan. *Transgender History*. Berkeley, CA: Seal Press, 2008.

Stryker, Susan, and Stephen Whittle, eds. *The Transgender Studies Reader*. London: Routledge, 2006.

Wiesner-Hanks, Merry E. *Gender in History: Global Perspectives*. 2nd ed. Oxford: Blackwell, 2010.

On Teaching

Berkin, Carol, ed. *Clio in the Classroom: A Guide to Teaching U.S. Women's History*. New York: Oxford University Press, 2009.

Lehman, Rosemary M., and Simone C. O. Conceiçao. *Creating a Sense of Presence in Online Teaching: How to "Be There" for Distance Learners*. San Francisco: Jossey-Bass, 2010.

Levesque, Stephane. *Thinking Historically: Educating Students for the Twenty-First Century*. Toronto: University of Toronto Press, 2008.

Light, Tracy Penny, Jane Nicholas, and Renee Bondy, eds. *Feminist Pedagogy in Higher Education: Critical Theory and Practice*. Waterloo, Ontario: Wilfrid Laurier University Press, 2015.

Strasser, Ulrike, and Heidi Tinsman. "Engendering World History." *Radical History Review* 91 (Winter 2005): 151–165.

Strasser, Ulrike, and Heidi Tinsman. "It's a Man's World? World History Meets History of Masculinity, in Latin American Studies for Instance." *Journal of World History* 21(1) (2010): 75–96.

Wiesner-Hanks, Merry. "Women's History and World History Courses." *Radical History Review* 91 (Winter 2005): 133–150.

Key Theoretical Works

Bennett, Judith. *History Matters: Patriarchy and the Challenge of Feminism*. Philadelphia: University of Pennsylvania Press, 2006.

Burton, Antoinette. "The Body in/as World History." In *A Companion to World History*, edited by Douglas Northrop, 272–284. Malden, MA: Wiley-Blackwell, 2012.

Butler, Judith. *Gender Trouble: Feminism and the Subversion of Identity*. 2nd ed. New York: Routledge, 2000.

Butler, Judith. *Undoing Gender*. London: Routledge, 2004.

Canaday, Margot, Marc Epprecht, Joanne Meyerowitz, Dagmar Herzog, Tamara Loos, Leslie Peirce, and Pete Sigal. "*American Historical Review* Forum: Transnational Sexualities." *American Historical Review* 114(5) (2009): 1250–1353.

Fausto-Sterling, Anne. *Sexing the Body: Gender Politics and the Construction of Sexuality*. New York: Basic Books, 2000.

Finlay, Robert. "The Refashioning of Martin Guerre." *American Historical Review* 93(3) (June 1988): 553–571, with a reply by Natalie Zemon Davis, "On the Lame," *American Historical Review* 93(3) (June 1988): 572–603.

"Forum: Rethinking Key Concepts in Gender History." *Gender and History* 28(2) (August 2016): 299–366.

Grewal, Inderpal, and Caren Kaplan. "Global Identities: Theorizing Transnational Studies of Sexuality." *GLQ: A Journal of Gay and Lesbian Studies* 7(4) (2001): 663–679.

Halperin, David. *How to Do the History of Homosexuality*. Chicago: University of Chicago Press, 2002.

Higginbotham, Evelyn Brooks. "African American Women's History and the Metalanguage of Race." *Signs* 17 (1992): 251–274.

"Intersectionality: Theorizing Power, Empowering Theory." *Signs* 38(4) (Summer 2013): 785–1055.

Meyerowitz, Joanne, Heidi Tinsman, Maria Bucur, Dyan Elliott, Gail Hershatter, Wang Zheng, and Joan Scott. "*American Historical Review* Forum: Revisiting 'Gender: A Useful Category of Historical Analysis.'" *American Historical Review* 113(5) (2008): 1344–1430.

Mohanty, Chandra Talpade. *Feminism without Borders: Decolonizing Theory, Practicing Solidarity*. Durham, NC: Duke University Press, 2003.

Nash, Jennifer C. "Re-thinking Intersectionality." *Feminist Review* 89 (June 2008): 1–15.

Riley, Denise. *"Am I That Name?": Feminism and the Category of "Women" in History*. Minneapolis: University of Minnesota Press, 1988.

Scott, Joan. "Gender: A Useful Category of Historical Analysis." *American Historical Review* 91 (1986): 1053–1075.

Spivak, Gayatri. "Can the Subaltern Speak?" In *Marxism and the Interpretation of Culture*, edited by Cary Nelson and Lawrence Grossberg, 271–316. Urbana-Champaign: University of Illinois Press, 1988.

"Thinking Sex/Thinking Gender." Special issue of *GLQ* 10(2) (2004): 211–313.

Essay Collections

Ballantyne, Tony, and Antoinette Burton, eds. *Bodies in Contact: Rethinking Colonial Encounters in World History*. Durham, NC: Duke University Press, 2005.

Basu, Amrita, ed. *Women's Movements in the Global Era: The Power of Local Feminisms*. Boulder, CO: Westview, 2010.

Chaudhuri, Nupur, Sherry J. Katz, and Mary Elizabeth Perry, eds. *Contesting Archives: Finding Women in the Sources*. Urbana-Champaign: University of Illinois Press, 2010.

Clancy-Smith, Julia, and Frances Gouda, eds. *Race, Gender, and Family Life in French and Dutch Colonialism*. Charlottesville: University Press of Virginia, 1998.

Davidoff, Leonore, Keith McCleland, and Eleni Varikas, eds. *Gender and History: Retrospect and Prospect*. Oxford: Blackwell, 2000.

Ekine, Sokari, and Hakima Abbas, eds. *Queer African Reader*. Nairobi: Pambazuka Press, 2013.

Gluck, Sherna Berger, and Daphne Patai, eds. *Women's Words: The Feminist Practice of Oral History*. New York: Routledge, 1991.

Mohanty, Chandra, Ann Russo, and Lourdes Torres, eds. *Third World Women and the Politics of Feminism*. Bloomington: Indiana University Press, 1991.

Patton, Cindy, and Benigno Sánchez-Eppler, eds. *Queer Diasporas*. Durham, NC: Duke University Press, 2000.

Smith, Bonnie G., ed. *Global Feminism since 1945*. London: Routledge, 2000.

Voland, Eckard Anthanasios Chasiotis, and Wulf Schiefenhovel, eds. *Grandmotherhood: The Evolutionary Significance of the Second Half of Female Life*. New Brunswick, NJ: Rutgers University Press, 2005.

Monographs

Abu-Lughod, Lila. *Remaking Women: Feminism and Modernity in the Middle East*. Princeton, NJ: Princeton University Press, 1997.

Brown, Peter. *The Body and Society: Men, Women and Sexual Renunciation in Early Christianity*. 2nd ed. New York: Columbia University Press, 2008.

Burton, Antoinette. *Dwelling in the Archive: Women Writing House, Home, and History in Late Colonial India*. Oxford: Oxford University Press, 2003.

Carrera, Magal M. *Imagining Identity in New Spain: Race, Lineage, and the Colonial Body in Portraiture and Casta Paintings*. Austin: University of Texas Press, 2003.

Chant, Sylvia, with Nikki Chase. *Gender in Latin America*. New Brunswick, NJ: Rutgers University Press, 2002.

Chauncey, George. *Gay New York: Gender, Urban Culture, and the Making of the Gay Male World, 1890–1940*. New York: Basic Books, 1995.

Davis, Natalie Zemon. *The Return of Martin Guerre*. Cambridge, MA: Harvard University Press, 1983.

Foxhall, Lin. *Studying Gender in Classical Antiquity*. New York: Cambridge University Press, 2013.

Getz, Trevor R., and Liz Clarke. *Abina and the Important Men: A Graphic History*. 2nd ed. New York: Oxford University Press, 2015.

Gilmartin, Christina Kelley. *Engendering the Chinese Revolution: Radical Women, Communist Politics, and Mass Movements in the 1920s*. Berkeley: University of California Press, 1995.

Ha, Marie-Paule. *French Women and the Empire: The Case of Indochina*. New York: Oxford University Press, 2014.

Hinsche, Bret. *Masculinities in Chinese History*. London: Rowman and Littlefield, 2013.

Hrdy, Sarah Blaffer. *Mothers and Others: The Evolutionary Origins of Mutual Understanding*. Cambridge, MA: Belknap, 2009.

Lanser, Susan. *The Sexuality of History: Modernity and the Sapphic, 1565–1830*. Chicago: University of Chicago Press, 2014.

Magubane, Zine. *Bringing the Empire Home: Race, Class, and Gender in Britain and Colonial South Africa*. Chicago: University of Chicago Press, 2004.

Mangan, Jane E. *Transatlantic Obligations: Creating the Bonds of Family in Conquest-Era Peru and Spain*. New York: Oxford University Press, 2016.

Mann, Susan L. *Gender and Sexuality in Modern Chinese History*. Cambridge: Cambridge University Press, 2011.

Moghadam, Valentine M. *Globalizing Women: Transnational Feminist Networks*. Baltimore, MD: Johns Hopkins University Press, 2005.

Najmabadi, Afsaneh. *Women with Mustaches and Men without Beards: Gender and Sexual Anxieties of Iranian Modernity*. Berkeley: University of California Press, 2005.

Pascoe, Peggy. *What Comes Naturally: Miscegenation Law and the Making of Race in America*. New York: Oxford University Press, 2010.

Powers, Jonathan. *A Bull of a Man: Images of Masculinity, Sex, and the Body in Indian Buddhism*. Cambridge, MA: Harvard University Press, 2009.

Rupp, Leila. *Worlds of Women: The Making of an International Women's Movement*. Princeton, NJ: Princeton University Press, 1997.

Salisbury, Joyce E. *Rome's Christian Empress: Galla Placida Rules at the Twilight of the Empire*. Baltimore, MD: Johns Hopkins University Press, 2015.

Sangado, Nirmala S. *Buddhist Nuns and Gendered Practice: In Search of the Female Renunciate*. New York: Oxford University Press, 2013.

Sensbach, Jon F. *Rebecca's Revival: Creating Black Christianity in the Atlantic World*. Cambridge, MA: Harvard University Press, 2005.

Stoler, Ann Laura. *Carnal Knowledge and Imperial Power: Race and the Intimate in Colonial Rule*. 2nd ed. Berkeley: University of California Press, 2011.

Traub, Valerie. *Thinking Sex with the Early Moderns*. Philadelphia: University of Pennsylvania Press, 2015.

Turshen, Meredeth. *Gender and the Political Economy of Conflict in Africa: The Persistence of Violence*. London: Routledge, 2016.

Valentine, David. *Imagining Transgender: An Ethnography of a Category*. Durham, NC: Duke University Press, 2007.

Wilson, Kathleen. *The Island Race: Englishness, Empire, and Gender in the Eighteenth Century*. London: Routledge, 2002.

Wilson, Liz. *Charming Cadavers: Horrific Figurations of the Feminine in Indian Buddhist Hagiographic Literature*. Chicago: University of Chicago Press, 1996.

Index

postcolonial theory and scholarship, 7, 11, 41, 47, 62, 73, 75

poststructuralism. *See* linguistic/cultural turn

presence in online learning, 79

prostitution, 50, 120

Protten, Rebecca, 95–96

public/private dichotomy, 45

Queer African Reader (Ekine and Abbas), 49, 50

Queer Diasporas (Patton and Sánchez-Eppler), 49

queer theory, 12–13, 19, 21, 34, 49, 105

quimbanda, 64

race, 7, 12, 23, 37, 46–47, 50–51, 60–62, 70, 73, 104

Race, Gender, and Family Life in French and Dutch Colonialism (Clancy-Smith and Gouda), 61

religion, 45, 58–60, 108. *See also* Christianity; Islamic culture

reproduction, 22, 31

research papers, 106–107

Return of Martin Guerre: book (Davis), 94; film, 94

Rich, Adrienne, 49

Rols, Bertrande de, 94, 109

Roman Empire, 19

Roy Rosenzweig Center for History and New Media (CHNM) at George Mason University, 18, 19, 72, 82

Rubin, Gayle, 42

same-sex relations, 6, 19, 23, 46, 91–92, 120

Sappho, 58

Sara Baartman and the Hottentot Venus: A Ghost Story and a Biography (Crais and Scully), 46

Schiebinger, Londa, 47

Scholarship on Teaching and Learning (SOTL), 101

science, 46–47, 93

Scott, Joan, 8, 43, 44

Sedgwick, Eve Kosofsky, 19, 49

Sei Shōnagon, 34

Sensbach, Jon, 95–96

sexuality, history of: courses in, 19–20, 23, 30–31; development of as a field, 6–8; modern, 19–20, 28, 31, 36

Sexuality in World History (Stearns), 20, 30

Shaarawi, Huda, 76

shamans, 63–64

Sharing the World Stage: Biography and Gender in World History (Slaughter et al.), 32

Sibtu of Mari, 32

Sinha, Mrinalini, 47

slavery and enslaved people, 21, 35–36, 47, 48, 57, 70, 73, 108

sources, primary, 4, 15, 20, 34, 39, 48, 58, 71–72, 76, 81–82, 98, 103–111, 115

South Africa, 60–61

Spivak, Gayatri, 7, 15, 48

Stearns, Peter, 19, 20

Strasser, Ulrike, 21, 62

student evaluations, 9, 111

Studying Gender in Classical Antiquity (Foxhall), 56

syllabi, 3, 5, 24–25, 72, 82, 100, 102, 112

textbooks, 8, 18, 31, 35, 44, 55, 116–117

theater, 118

theory, gender and feminist, 41–42, 71, 98. *See also* queer theory

third gender categories, 12, 15, 63–64, 74

Third Sex, Third Gender (Herdt), 46

Thornton, John, 36